NOTES AND ANECDOTES
OF MANY YEARS

From a photograph copyright by Underwood & Underwood.

Joseph Bucklin Bishop

NOTES AND ANECDOTES
OF MANY YEARS

BY
JOSEPH BUCKLIN BISHOP

Friends are the sunshine of life.
—JOHN HAY.

Essay Index Reprint Series

BOOKS FOR LIBRARIES PRESS
FREEPORT, NEW YORK

First Published 1925
Reprinted 1970

INTERNATIONAL STANDARD BOOK NUMBER:
0-8369-1904-1

LIBRARY OF CONGRESS CATALOG CARD NUMBER:
78-128210

PRINTED IN THE UNITED STATES OF AMERICA

TO
THE MEMORY OF
MY DEARLY LOVED DAUGHTER
ALICE BISHOP
CHEERING AND HELPING COMRADE OF
MANY YEARS

AUTHOR'S NOTE

Some of the material in this book was published in another form several years ago, but it has been revised and many additions to it have been made. A few of the anecdotes of Roosevelt, Hay, and others have also been used in other of my publications, but they are reproduced here in order to make the narrative a complete record.

J. B. B.

CONTENTS

CHAPTER		PAGE
I.	A Plea for Anecdotage	1
II.	"The Tribune" and Horace Greeley	8
III.	The Tragic Greeley Campaign	25
IV.	Two Famous Preachers	35
V.	John Hay	44
VI.	Isaac H. Bromley—William Winter	68
VII.	Edwin L. Godkin	87
VIII.	Theodore Roosevelt	111
IX.	Theodore Roosevelt—Continued	135
X.	Friends of Many Kinds	156
XI.	Maj.-Gen. George W. Goethals	187
	Index	229

NOTES AND ANECDOTES
OF MANY YEARS

CHAPTER I

A PLEA FOR ANECDOTAGE

MANY years ago, in reading "Lothair," I came across this remark, placed by Disraeli in the mouth of one of his characters: "When a man falls into his anecdotage it is a sign for him to retire from the world." I was much younger then than I am now, but the word "anecdotage" was new to me, and the sting in its tail, if I may so define its effect, made a lasting impression upon my mind. This impression became a distinct chill when I later contemplated a proposal to record some of the many anecdotes and episodes which linger in my memory, and which I have cherished with affection as marking the most enjoyable experiences of my life. Should I, by making such a record, demonstrate that I had fallen into my anecdotage and ought to retire in silence from the world? The thought was a disturbing one, and as I was turning it over in my mind, with an underlying feeling of resentment for the man who invented the word, I discerned, quite by accident, that it was fully

NOTES AND ANECDOTES

a century old when the author of "Lothair" had used it, and that he had borrowed it from his father, Isaac Disraeli, who had quoted it many years earlier and had not been alarmed by it in the least. This discovery prompted me to a hunt for the inventor of the word, with the ultimate result of enabling me to look upon it with more equanimity than had previously been possible.

In a preface which he wrote to an edition of his "Curiosities of Literature," published in 1839, Isaac Disraeli said: "Among my earliest literary friends, two distinguished themselves by their anecdotal literature: James Petit Andrews, by his 'Anecdotes Ancient and Modern,' and William Seward by his 'Anecdotes of Distinguished Persons.' These volumes were favorably received, and to such a degree, that a wit of that day, who is still a wit as well as a poet, considered that we were far gone in our anecdotage." The first named of the two books was published in 1789 and the second in 1795, so that the word must have made its first appearance in the latter part of the eighteenth century. In the same edition of the work of the elder Disraeli to which I have referred, there appears a memoir of that author by Benjamin Disraeli, and in this the son alludes

A PLEA FOR ANECDOTAGE

to the remark quoted by his father and names as the poet and wit who made it "Mr. Rogers," meaning presumably Samuel Rogers.

This seems to me to fix the parentage of the word with reasonable accuracy, but I find no reference to the elder Disraeli as an authority for it in any of the leading dictionaries or literary reference books. The New English Dictionary says it "is attributed to John Wilkes," but gives no quotation in support of that assertion. Rogers might have borrowed it from Wilkes, who antedated him many years as a writer, but if such was the case it is surprising that the elder Disraeli, who was a marvel in tracing such matters to their sources, was not aware of it. De Quincey used it in 1823 in passages quoted in several dictionaries, and in one a writer in 1880 is cited who speaks of "a man who has reached his anecdotage—to use a pun which Disraeli the younger has conveyed from Wilkes." This is an error. The citations I have made from Disraeli's memoir of his father show clearly that he conveyed it from him.

The depressing aspect of the word, to any one who loves anecdotes and has a disposition to relate or record them, lies in the definitions which the dictionaries give of it. The most usual is:

"Suggested by age and dotage; garrulous old age." This is undoubtedly the sense in which the inventor used it, and also the sense in which it has been most commonly used since. It may have deterred some timid possessors of valuable anecdotal treasures from displaying them for the delight of the world, but happily it had no terrors for the elder Disraeli. In the preface in which he quotes it he speaks of Doctor Johnson as "a famished man for anecdotal literature," who "sorely complained of the penury of our literary history," and then gives this interesting explanation of the principle upon which he constructed those works which take first rank in the anecdotal literature of all times: "An induction from a variety of particulars seemed to me to combine that delight which Johnson derived from anecdotes with that philosophy which Bolinbroke founded on examples; and on this principle the last three volumes of the 'Curiosities of Literature' were constructed, freed from the formality of dissertation and the vagueness of the lighter essay."

In his chapter on "Literary Anecdotes," in one of these volumes, Disraeli says: "How superficial is that cry of some impertinent pretended geniuses of these times who affect to exclaim, 'Give me no anecdotes of an author, but give me his works.'

A PLEA FOR ANECDOTAGE

I have often found the anecdotes more interesting than the works."

In conversation with John Hay a few years before his death, I cited this utterance in support of something that he was saying to the same effect, whereupon he added (I quote from memory): "Real history is not to be found in books, but in the personal anecdotes and private letters of those who make history. These reveal the men themselves and the motives that actuate them, and give us also their estimate of those who are associated with them. No one should ever destroy a private letter that contains light on public men, or willingly let die an illuminating anecdote disclosing their individuality."

Doctor Johnson died before the word anecdotage was invented, but it is a safe assumption that he would not have been disturbed by it in his avowed love of anecdotes. "Give us as many anecdotes as you can," said he to Boswell, whom he was urging to write an account of his visit to Corsica; "I love anecdotes." In his dictionary he defined anecdote as "something yet unpublished, secret history"; and in a later edition he added: "It is now used, after the French, for a biographical incident; a minute passage of private life."

NOTES AND ANECDOTES

Little did the doctor think when he was setting down those meanings that the fullest and most complete exemplification of the uttermost possibilities of the meaning of the word would be found in the immortal biography of his own life by the inimitable and incomparable Boswell who had, says Augustine Birrell, "always floating through his fuddled brain a great deal of portraiture." In discussing Boswell's method, Mr. Birrell, after remarking that the world has been talking of Doctor Johnson for more than a century, goes on to say:

> What does this perpetual interest in Dr. Johnson prove? Why, nothing whatever, except that he was interesting. But this is a great deal; indeed, it is the whole matter for a man, a woman, or a book. When you come to think of it, it is our sole demand.
>
> But how does it come about that we can all at this distance of time be so infatuated about a man who was not a great philosopher or poet, but only a miscellaneous writer? The answer must be, Johnson's is a transmitted personality. . . . But whether we read the "Biography" or the "Memoirs," it cannot escape our notice that Johnson's personality has been transmitted to us chiefly by a record of his *talk*.

What was Boswell's record of Doctor Johnson's talk but a huge bundle of anecdotes of the

A PLEA FOR ANECDOTAGE

man himself, and in lesser, but no slight degree, of his associates? The whole Johnson coterie live before us as we read, and endlessly re-read, with never-flagging delight, one of the most, if not the most, inexhaustibly interesting of all books in literature.

Fortified by these high authorities, I am emboldened to run the risk of being adjudged a victim of the old-age infirmity of anecdotage, and shall endeavor in the following pages to depict, through aid of incident and anecdote, the personality of men, most of them famous, whom it has been my high privilege to know, many of whom have honored me with their friendship and confidence. Of the anecdotes that I shall record, I feel justified in saying that all of them are reasonably authentic and most of them are based upon my personal knowledge. Time and the fallibility of human memory may have put extra touches upon some of them, but I shall cite none that I do not believe to be veracious, fully mindful of the human tendency in the relating of anecdotes to do what Prosper in "The Tempest" says Antonio did: "Made such a sinner of his memory to credit his own lie."

CHAPTER II

THE TRIBUNE AND HORACE GREELEY

A FEW months after graduation from Brown University in 1870, I went to New York City and entered the service of *The Tribune* as a reporter. In those days the editorial office of *The Tribune* was a thoroughly democratic place. It was situated in the fourth story of an old ramshackle five-story building, on the site later more than covered by a towering edifice, and consisted of the most thoroughly ill-furnished and ill-kept suite of rooms imaginable. There was scarcely a desk in any one of them that had not been for many years in a state of well-nigh hopeless decrepitude, and scarcely a chair with a full complement of its original legs, the place of the missing member or two being supplied often with a piece of board nailed to the side. There were only about half enough chairs and desks to go round. Reporters, and even editors, were obliged to take turns in writing their "copy," and secured a share in a desk only after a considerable period of service. One of my earliest recollections of the edi-

THE TRIBUNE AND HORACE GREELEY

torial room is of hearing Isaac H. Bromley say to Clarence Cook, the genial, gentle, and delightful friend, but most merciless of art critics: "Cook, are you through with that desk? If you are, scrape off the blood and feathers and let me come."

The editorial room fronted on Printing House Square, and was entered through the reporters' room. A half-partition of wood and glass, the latter very dirty and never washed, separated the two. It was only eight feet or more in height, but, low as it was, to the minds of the reporters it was the most formidable of barriers. They regarded that front room as the very heaven of their aspirations. They looked with admiration and envy upon the men—Doctor George Ripley, Bayard Taylor, William Winter, John R. G. Hassard, and John Hay among them—who walked daily through the city room into it. For, ill-furnished and ill-kept as was *The Tribune* office of those days, it harbored a moral and intellectual spirit that I met nowhere else during my thirty-five years of journalistic experience. Every member of the force, from reporter to editor, regarded it as a great privilege to be on *The Tribune* and to write for its columns, and that there could be no higher ambition than to write for the same page as that for which Horace Greeley wrote. All the reporters who were ambitious studied that page with care daily, seeking to imbibe its spirit and to fit themselves by reading and practice to write ultimately for it. They became familiar with the styles of the different contributors to it, and discussed their relative merits with the enthusiasm and assurance of youth.

Through the always open and unguarded doorway of the editorial rooms there drifted in and out at will a curiously incongruous throng of "uplifters," or reformers, and intellectuals. The former consisted mainly of left-overs of anti-slavery days, surviving abolitionists who came to see Mr. Greeley to get his editorial support for their "causes" and his pecuniary support for their material wants. Among the intellectuals were Edmund Clarence Stedman, Richard H. Stoddard, Charles Dudley Warner, Thomas Bailey Aldrich, Bret Harte, and Joaquin Miller. The two groups did not intermingle, for they had nothing in common, nor did the members of the editorial staff hold more than casual intercourse with Mr. Greeley's visitors.

The quaintest figure in the place was that of the great editor, Horace Greeley, careless and dishevelled in dress, as if he had put on his clothes in the dark, with the round and rosy face of a child and a cherubic expression of simplicity and gentleness. At the time of which I am speaking he occupied a small room on the second floor of the building, access to which was by means of a blind stairway leading from the counting-room.

There were legends innumerable of his eccentricities, most of which were, I am confident, reasonably authentic. The one which antedated all others was narrated to me by Charles T. Congdon, who had won much contemporary fame as an editorial writer for the paper in the anti-slavery days, and a selection of whose writings was published in book form by J. S. Redfield in 1869 under the title of "Tribune Essays."

During the draft riots in New York in 1863, which began on the 13th of July and continued with great fury for four days, the Tribune Building was one of the first points of attack. A mob which had been gathering in front of it during the first day began an assault late in the afternoon of the 13th, broke the windows in the lower stories, sacked and set fire to the publication office, and would have destroyed the entire structure had not the police and firemen appeared early on the scene. Fearing attack, the publisher of the paper, early in the day, had secured some hand-grenades with which to repel it. According to Mr. Congdon, Mr. Greeley, on entering the general editorial room occupied by the assistant editors, discovered a pile of these lying near a window. He demanded, in his high-pitched and rather squeaky voice, what they were and why they were there. When informed that they were hand-grenades and were to be thrown out to drive off the mob in case it attacked the building, he cried: "Take 'em away, take 'em away! I don't want to kill anybody, and besides they're damn sight more likely to go off and kill some of us! Take 'em away, I say!" They were removed, and Mr. Greeley went into the adjoining small room which he occupied at that time, and began writing as if nothing unusual was happening, although the square in front of the building was packed with an ugly-looking, shouting mob, making repeated demonstrations of hostility toward it.

Mr. Greeley wrote steadily on till his lunch time arrived, when he arose, put on his hat, and started to go out. Oliver Johnson, his tried and devoted associate of many years, rushed forward, grabbed him by the arm, saying: "Where are you going?" "To get my dinner, of course," was the calm reply. "You take your life in your hand if you go out there," exclaimed Johnson in great excitement. Turning his beaming smile fully upon him, Mr. Greeley in perfect quiet said: "No I don't, Oliver, no I don't. Besides, if I can't eat my dinner when I'm hungry my life isn't worth anything to me!" He turned about, went down-stairs, opened the front door of the building, and, stepping out upon the broad, flat stone which constituted the doorstep, looked calmly over the throng which stood in solid mass in front of him. When the rioters saw him standing there in his familiar white hat, with his head tilted slightly backward to bring his spectacles into focus, and with his childlike smile, they became suddenly silent. He stepped down among them, they stood apart as he advanced, opening a line through which he walked to his destination, unmolested by angry speech or act.

Mr. Greeley's contemporaries, who took unceasing delight in misrepresenting and ridiculing him, did not give him credit for this act of genuine courage. *The World* declared two days later that the editor of *The Tribune* "had not dared to enter his office, but remained trembling all day long in the safe umbrage of a friendly restaurant, escaping at last under cover of darkness to his home." It repeated the assertion on the third

NOTES AND ANECDOTES

day, whereupon Mr. Greeley made this unusually restrained but none the less characteristic rejoinder, quoting the charge:

There must be a stop to this. Briefly, then, the editor of *The Tribune* came to his office on Monday morning at 9 o'clock, walking to it from a Harlem car in plain sight of scores; remained at his work till dinner time; then walked deliberately through the crowd to Windust's, ate his dinner, and at once took a carriage thence to his lodging, in broad daylight and with no sort of concealment or disguise. He prevented the arming of *The Tribune* office until after the assault upon, sack and attempt to burn it that evening; then he thought the time had come for decisive measures; and the next morning (Tuesday) he devoted mainly to aiding to put it in fighting trim; coming again openly by car down town, walking from the car through the crowd to his office, and remaining there from 9 a.m. to 4 p.m., when he walked away undisguised and unassailed as before. Yesterday he was seen again at the office at 10 a.m., coming in a carriage because there was no public conveyance and spending the day about his business as usual. (N.B.—The fighting arrangements did not require renewal.) He left at a proper dinner hour as before and expects to be back at his post in good season this morning. And if *The World* will advise its friends not to devastate the dwellings of inoffensive people who kindly watched over him in sickness two years ago, and with whom he has never "boarded" since, and who are nowise related to him, it will be all the favor he asks from that *quarter.**

**The Tribune, July 16, 1863.

THE TRIBUNE AND HORACE GREELEY

It will be observed that Mr. Greeley's diary of his movements affords confirmatory evidence of the accuracy of Mr. Congdon's narrative.

The allusion in the closing passages to the devastation of dwellings of inoffensive people was to the sacking of the house of John S. Gibbons in 29th Street, on the first day of the riots. Mr. Gibbons was a Hicksite Quaker and prominent Abolitionist, who was at one time an editor of the *Anti-Slavery Standard*. He won title to enduring fame as the author of the stirring war-song:

> "We are coming, Father Abraham,
> Three hundred thousand more."

The song was published anonymously in 1862 in the New York *Evening Post,* of which William Cullen Bryant was editor, and for a considerable period the authorship was attributed to Mr. Bryant, who subsequently gave public credit for it to Mr. Gibbons. It was set to music by one of the famous Hutchinson family of singers, and was one of the most popular of all the martial songs of the Civil War. Mr. Gibbons had excited attention and much indignation among the anti-abolitionist elements in his neighborhood by illuminating his house when President Lincoln's Emancipation Proclamation was issued, and his front

NOTES AND ANECDOTES

doorway had been besmirched with coal-tar at that time. He was known to be a personal friend of Mr. Greeley, who visited him frequently and who had been cared for there during a period of illness. The rioters shouted that it was "Greeley's boarding place," though he had never boarded there, and assaulted it with great violence. Mr. Gibbons and two daughters took refuge in the house next door, and through its skylight passed over the roofs of other houses to Eighth Avenue, where Joseph H. Choate, an intimate friend of the family, had a carriage in waiting for them.

It was subsequent to the riots that Mr. Greeley began his occupancy of the down-stairs room leading from the publication office. It was a small room, nearly filled with the large roller-top desk at which he wrote habitually. He was very near-sighted and wrote with his face very close to the paper. His absorption in his work was so complete that considerable effort was necessary to draw his attention away from it, and any one accosting him was generally compelled to wait until he had reached the end of, or a stopping place in, the article he was composing.

Many anecdotes were told in the office, of incidents in that little room, a few of which I will

THE TRIBUNE AND HORACE GREELEY

venture to record, selecting those which I believe to be authentic.

On one occasion, during a crisis in city politics, *The Tribune* had refused to support the party ticket and had thereby aroused the furious wrath of a party leader. This person, from long and familiar intercourse, knew the way to the little room and was accustomed to enter it without ceremony. On this occasion he burst through the door and began a torrent of abuse immediately, standing over the bowed figure of the editor and pouring it upon him at close range. He accused him of being a traitor to his party, of working its ruin and that of the city, and of other similar crimes. Mr. Greeley, who had been writing when he entered, wrote steadily on, showing no sign of consciousness of his presence. The visitor, his wrath increased by this inattention, shouted louder than ever and enhanced the vigor of his epithets. Still the editor wrote on. The visitor took a turn of the little room, came back to the desk and said it all over again. Still the editor wrote on. Twice or more times he repeated this performance, always with the same result—the editor wrote on. Thoroughly exhausted in wrath and language, he at length opened the door to depart. As he was closing it, the pen of the editor slackened slowly,

NOTES AND ANECDOTES

then stopped, and glancing over his shoulder, with his face wreathed in a childlike smile, Mr. Greeley said soothingly: "Don't go! Don't go! Come back and *free your mind!*"

On another occasion a gentleman of wealth and standing in the community had taken umbrage at some observations which *The Tribune* had made concerning some project with which he was identified. He was a pompous person, endowed with a generous sense of his own importance. He visited the office and asked to see Mr. Greeley, handing his card to the office-boy and insisting, although the boy had told him that a card was unnecessary, that it be presented in advance of himself. The boy went first with the card and placed it on the desk beside Mr. Greeley, who was writing in his usual manner. The visitor followed and, as he entered the room, he saluted the back of Mr. Greeley's head with a vigorous "Good morning!" No response or sign of recognition coming from the editor, who continued to write, the visitor took a turn of the room, stepped to the side of the desk, and in a loud tone said: "Good morning, Mr. Greeley!" Still no pause and no response. He took another turn, came again to the desk, and, with visibly rising wrath, fairly shouted: "Good morning, Mr. Greeley!" Still

THE TRIBUNE AND HORACE GREELEY

getting no response, his slight hold on his temper slipped, and he exclaimed: "Mr. Greeley, I have sent my card to you, like a gentleman. I have spoken to you three times, like a gentleman. Now if you continue to pay no attention to me I shall be obliged to conclude that *you* are no gentleman!" The moving finger ceased to write, and with an amused smile on his cherubic face, the editor looked up a moment and asked: "Well, who in thunder ever said I was?" Mr. Pomposity was so astounded that he forgot both his anger and his errand, and as Mr. Greeley resumed writing immediately, he quietly went away.

This was his usual method with troublesome callers and it was invariably successful. Nobody ever knew whether or not he had a quiet chuckle with himself after they had gone, for he made no allusion to such incidents.

He was subjected constantly to demands for loans, contributions to societies and charities, and for aid to "causes," for it was notorious that he was an "easy mark." An assistant editor who went to consult him on a matter connected with the paper found a lady sitting by his desk importuning him for a contribution to a charity, undismayed by his conduct in writing away without paying heed to what she was saying. As the assistant editor entered, Mr. Greeley threw down his pen and, leaning across the lady so closely as to crowd her against the wall, put his mouth to a speaking-tube above her head and shouted into it: "Sam, Sam, for God's sake send me up five dollars and let me get rid of this pesky woman!" Sam was Mr. Sinclair, publisher of the paper, and the speaking-tube led directly to his desk. The money came up, Mr. Greeley, without a word, handed it to the lady, who departed unperturbed. She had obviously visited him before.

His gifts of money to beggars of all sorts and of the most obvious humbug character were notorious, and called forth repeated protests from his associates. His excuse was always the same: "There's one chance in a thousand that my gift may do the poor devil some good, and I'm not willing to lose that chance." He lent something like seventy-five thousand dollars, with no security whatever, to a spendthrift son of one of the earlier Vanderbilts, and when the boy's father said to him: "You think I'll pay the money back to you, but I won't." "Well, who in thunder asks you to pay it?" replied Greeley. After the editor's death, when it was found that he had left only a small estate, the boy's father paid the money over to Mr. Greeley's daughters.

THE TRIBUNE AND HORACE GREELEY

Mr. Congdon told me that it was a frequent occurrence for Mr. Greeley to enter the editorial room brandishing the morning issue of the paper and demanding, pointing to an article in it, "What damn fool wrote that?" If some one replied, "I did, Mr. Greeley," his apparent anger would evaporate, and with the usual smile he would say, "Oh, you did!" and say no more about it.

If any member of the force made a blunder or was guilty of an inaccuracy in a published statement, he was very likely to order his immediate discharge. In making up some items of political news shortly after I had been promoted to the editorial staff, I wrote that the Republican majority in an election in a county of a Western State had been 12,000, that being the figure given in a newspaper of the locality. On the afternoon of the day on which the item was published, the managing editor handed me a three-page note written to him by Mr. Greeley, in which my instant dismissal was ordered on the ground that a man who was "so hopeless a fool as not to know that there were not 12,000 voters in that whole county was of no use in a newspaper office." It took me an hour or more to decipher the note—all that has been said about the illegibility of his handwriting is true—and when I discovered its verdict on my capacity I went to the managing editor in great alarm, asking if I was to go. He smiled at my fright, saying that Mr. Greeley was impulsive and did not quite mean all he said, that I need not go this time, but that I should be especially careful about election figures, since Mr. Greeley knew the voting strength of nearly every town, city, and county of the United States, and was intolerant of any inaccuracy in stating election returns. I learned subsequently that a man who was employed as exchange reader had been ordered "fired" by Mr. Greeley at frequent intervals for several years, but had never gone, and that on one occasion, when Mr. Greeley came upon him still at work in the office, he stood a moment looking at him, then smiled and, shaking his head, turned away.

Innumerable stories are told of his handwriting, one of which I know to be true. He had written an editorial article advocating the running of an early milk train from Westchester County to New York City. The compositor who usually put his manuscript in type was away, and the task was assigned to another who was unfamiliar with it. When the article appeared in print "early" was set up as "swill," and the consequence was an outbreak of furious wrath among

THE TRIBUNE AND HORACE GREELEY

the farmers of Westchester County, large delegations of whom descended upon the office to see Mr. Greeley. Their wrath was mildness itself in comparison with his. He obtained the name of the guilty compositor and wrote a letter to the foreman of the composing-room ordering his immediate discharge. The man asked to have the letter as a keepsake, and it was given to him. It was written on paper with *The Tribune* heading, and the only intelligible portion of it was the signature "Horace Greeley" at the bottom. The compositor went across the street and applied for work in *The Times* office. Asked where he had been employed and if he had a recommendation, he produced the letter and presented it as a certificate. It was accepted at its face value and the man given work, for nobody unacquainted with Mr. Greeley's chirography, which has been described as the "tracks of a drunken hen," could read it. The compositor retained it for years, always getting employment on it. Mr. Greeley heard of this result from time to time and was greatly amused by it.

A more whimsical, impracticable, lovable man never lived, and American journalism has produced few superiors to him as a clear and forcible editorial writer. He came very closely into Doc-

NOTES AND ANECDOTES

tor Johnson's estimate of Oliver Goldsmith: "No man was more foolish when he had not a pen in his hand, or more wise when he had." He was at the summit of his fame and influence when I entered *The Tribune* office in 1870, and the power that he wielded throughout the country was not equalled by any other editor at that time, neither has it been equalled by any editor since. I do not think this statement can be successfully questioned. *The Tribune* was a tremendous moral force in the land because of the personal faith of the plain people in the honesty of the editor. He was, in the minds of thousands, *The Tribune,* and every word it contained was believed implicitly because he was the man behind it. Shortly after his death, when I returned to my native town in New England, an old settler who had known me from childhood asked me: "What are you doing in New York now, Joseph?" When I replied that I was still with *The Tribune,* he exclaimed in great astonishment: "With *The Try-bune!* Does it print yet? I thought Greeley was dead!"

CHAPTER III

THE TRAGIC GREELEY CAMPAIGN

HOW anyone who had been associated with Mr. Greeley or was familiar with his personality could think of him as fit to be President of the United States, is incomprehensible. His nomination was simply the incredible first step in a pitiful tragedy. If he had not been the most simple-minded of men he would have realized it himself. But not only did he not realize it, but he believed in his inmost soul that he was the best man in the country for the nomination at the time. He was obsessed by the idea that he was the one man who could heal the wounds of the Civil War and bring the North and the South together at once. It never occurred to him that he was incapable of choosing wisely those who should become his advisers, in case he were elected, for he had no suspicion of his own helplessness in the hands of designing persons. He had never been startled into such a suspicion, apparently, by the extraordinary aggregation of "long-haired men and short-haired women" that for years had trooped through *The Tribune* office, collecting tribute steadily from him and "queering" him with all rational persons.

I recall vividly this aggregation, when, with swollen ranks, it swept over the office after his nomination. Recruits came from all quarters and as one surveyed them he was moved to exclaim, as the wife of a moderate American reformer once said to her husband: "Why, oh why, do the insane so cling to you?" In front, with flowing mane which he tossed back with what was known as the "leonine gesture" of his head, strode Theodore Tilton, saying to all comers: "It is glorious! I shall take the stump! I shall wear a white hat! We shall redeem the land." Close behind him came Tennie C. Claflin and Victoria Woodhull, advocates of what it would be base flattery to call social reforms, and a wild-eyed, dishevelled host that made Falstaff's army look like a crack regiment of regulars.

If Mr. Greeley was disturbed by this alarming army of disciples, he did not reveal the fact. It is a safe assertion that he perceived nothing either unusual or harmful in it. Under the careful grooming of his sane intimates he reformed his own dress with care, studiously eliminating those established marks of disorder that had character-

THE TRAGIC GREELEY CAMPAIGN

ized it for many years, and adopted as a daily garb a black swallow-tail coat and trousers, with a black velveteen waistcoat and a white muslin "string" necktie. He was photographed in this costume, sitting by the high desk at which he habitually wrote, with a quill pen in his hand, with the famous white hat visible near by, and Whitelaw Reid, his managing editor, standing looking down upon him. The photograph was circulated widely and attracted much attention. It was said of it by malicious persons that Mr. Reid was watching Mr. Greeley closely, ready to jump into the editor's chair in case he ventured to leave it. The likenesses of both men were excellent, but Mr. Greeley was so clearly "made up" for the occasion, so thoroughly "reformed" in dress, so obviously unfamiliar with the quill pen which had been placed in his hand and which he had never used and never would use, that the picture caused a good deal of amusement in *The Tribune* office as well as in journalistic circles generally.

It was, in fact, a very remarkable photograph, more remarkable possibly than it appeared to be at the time. Looking at it to-day, over an interval of fifty years and in the disillusioning light of history, it is easy to read in it a full and satisfactory explanation of the hopeless campaign which followed its publication. All the artificiality—sham is too strong a word—and all the sadness of the Greeley campaign are depicted there.

It was an artificial candidacy, for the Greeley that his supporters presented to the people was not the Greeley of *The Tribune*—simple, whimsical, impracticable, unlimited in gullibility, and grotesquely careless in dress. Not a single person among his supporters, possessing even average intelligence and truthfulness, could say honestly that he believed the genuine Greeley qualified to discharge with dignity and efficiency the duties of the Presidency. One and all of them knew at heart that he had nearly every disqualification for the office. They made unconscious confession of this when they sought to make him over, or make him up, for the campaign. Their justification for the attempted deceit was their belief that he would allow them to control and direct him in case of election.

He was no conscious party to the scheme. However insincere his chief promoters may have been, he was absolutely sincere in his belief that he was not only fit for the Presidency but better fitted to exercise its functions for the highest welfare of the country and all its people than any other man. Furthermore, he was confident at

THE TRAGIC GREELEY CAMPAIGN

the outset that the people had such complete faith in him that they would rejoice at the opportunity to elect him. It was the revelation of the fact that they did not have this full faith, that they could not trust him with the Presidency, that sent him to his grave a broken-hearted man.

How long his early confidence in his success endured cannot be known, but it was only for a short time. As early as September 10 he wrote to a lady friend with whom he was in regular and intimate correspondence: "I only write to say that I trust you will not care what the result of our Presidential combat may be. Just now, the skies look dark; a month hence they may be brighter; but in any case I shall be what I am, shall have less care out of than in office."

A day later, he wrote in a similar vein, saying, "defeat would have many consolations," adding with a characteristic touch of humor: "While there are doubts as to my fitness for President, nobody seems to deny that I would make a capital beaten candidate."

He realized a full month before election day that he was on a hopeless quest, for the verdict in the States which at that time held elections in October made any other view impossible.

On October 14 he wrote to his friend: "You

NOTES AND ANECDOTES

must not take our reverses to heart. I may soon have to shed some tears for my wife, who seems to be sinking at last, but I shall not give one to any possible result of the political canvass. I shall fight on to the end; but for you, please say with King Agur of old, 'The bitterness of death is past,' and think henceforth of less melancholy themes."

He continued the fight with heroic courage, making a stumping tour of the country and delivering a series of speeches notable for intellectual force and eloquence. He returned from the tour to take his seat by the bedside of his dying wife. That sad vigil ended with her death on October 30, and six days later came the overwhelming verdict of the nation against him at the polls. Heart-broken and weary, he made a desperate attempt to rally his forces and go forward, but the end had come. The bow had been stretched too often and too far, and snapped. The second day after election he announced in a card over his signature that he had returned to the editorship of *The Tribune*. He did return to the office, where he wrote or attempted to write three or four short editorial articles, but barely finished any of them, handing them to his assistant with the remark that there was in each of them an idea

THE TRAGIC GREELEY CAMPAIGN

that was worth developing, but he did not feel equal to the task of doing it himself.

He had been greatly distressed by an editorial article which appeared in *The Tribune,* on November 7, entitled "Crumbs of Comfort." This was written by John R. G. Hassard, for many years, both during Mr. Greeley's lifetime and subsequently, the principal editorial writer of the paper. He wrote it in order to give expression to a feeling of relief which pervaded the entire establishment with no suspicion that it would give offense. The passages which excited angry protest were the following:

> There has been no time, until now, within the last 12 years when *The Tribune* was not supposed to keep, for the benefit of the idle and incapable, a sort of Federal Employment Agency, established to get places under the government for those who were indisposed to work for their living. . . . Every red-nosed politician who had cheated at the caucus and fought at the polls looked to the editor of *The Tribune* to secure his appointment as gauger, or army chaplain, or as minister to France. At last we shall keep our office clear of blatherskites and political beggars and go about our daily work with the satisfaction of knowing that not the most credulous of place-hunters will suspect us of having any credit with the appointing powers.

Some of the old motley following of Mr.

NOTES AND ANECDOTES

Greeley appear to have recognized personal assault in the designations "red-nosed politicians," "blatherskites," and "political beggars," and exposed their pain to Mr. Greeley, insisting that he disavow and retract the article, which he attempted to do. An authentic account of this episode is given by John Bigelow, in an extract from his diary which he published in his "Retrospect of an Active Life":

Nov. 16, 1872. Whitelaw Reid breakfasted with me and told me a great deal about Greeley and *The Tribune*. Seems to think his position there depends upon Greeley's being there. Says Greeley was very indignant at the article entitled "Crumbs of Comfort" that appeared a day or two after election. He projected an article correcting it—it was written by Hassard—which if printed would have sent every editor out of the office. Reid suppressed it. Greeley even then cried and whined and went on like a baby. He called himself over and over again "a black fraud," said he was ruined, *The Tribune* was ruined, begged the trustees to turn him out, turn Reid out, turn any one out to save the paper.

Mr. Greeley's mental condition at the time was revealed in a letter to his friend, on November 8:

I am indeed most wretched. As to my wife's death, I do not lament it. Her sufferings were so terrible that I rather felt relieved when she peacefully slept the long sleep. I did not shed a tear. In fact, I am far beyond

THE TRAGIC GREELEY CAMPAIGN

tears. Nor do I care for defeat, however crushing. I dread only the malignity with which I am hounded, and the possibility that it may ruin *The Tribune*. My enemies mean to kill that; if they would only kill me instead, I would thank them lovingly. And so many of my old friends hate me for what I have done that life seems too hard to bear.

He was, in fact, on the verge of mental as well as physical collapse at the time, and a few days later was taken to the house of a physician near his farm in Westchester County where he developed inflammation of the brain and died on November 29.

It has been said that he was insane at the end, but this was true only in the sense that he was delirious from his malady. The news of his death made a profound impression upon the country. From all parts of the land, through the pulpit and press and in public speech came a great volume of tributes of honor and affectionate regard to which a tinge of pity, perhaps of remorse, gave a deep and unwonted note of tenderness. The campaign had been marked by unusual brutality in speech and print and caricature, and Mr. Greeley had been the worst sufferer from it. His tragic death, under conditions of such acute pathos, moved the nation into what

NOTES AND ANECDOTES

appeared to be a spontaneous impulse to set itself right with him, to show that while the American people could not trust him with the Presidency, their faith in him and their affection for him remained undiminished. He went to his grave sad with the belief that many of his old friends had come to hate him. This could not have been true, for no man, friend or foe, could hate that simple, honest soul.

CHAPTER IV

TWO FAMOUS PREACHERS

WHEN I began my journalistic career as a reporter there were two clergymen who held front rank as orators both in their profession and outside of it,—Henry Ward Beecher and Doctor E. H. Chapin, one a Congregationalist and the other a Universalist. In the course of my duties I heard both quite frequently on various occasions, sometimes separately, at other times pitted against each other. I was a youth just out of college, very impressionable and enthusiastic, and the two men, both of whom were far superior in intellectual ability and oratorical gifts to any one with whom I had previously come in contact, made a great impression upon me.

Mr. Beecher, especially, interested and delighted me. His humor which was always bubbling forth, and his complete human sympathy and understanding, were the chief elements of attraction. I have never heard a preacher who could be compared with him for a moment, for his method was his own and totally unlike any other within my experience. He did not so much preach as talk—and most entertaining talk it was.

NOTES AND ANECDOTES

I never heard a word of doctrine from him. The subject was always the same,—life and its problems and trials—human ills and weaknesses—human frailties and sources of strength. The religion that he preached was that of daily life, not a creed but a practice, not abstract morality, but personal, individual conduct.

The scene in Plymouth church in the days of his supreme power was a most impressive one. The auditorium was a huge barn-like room holding several thousands of people. There were deep galleries on three sides, and at the pulpit end, back of the simple stand at which Mr. Beecher spoke, there was a choir of at least a hundred voices. To the ends of all the pews on the main floor folding chairs were affixed and when these were let down the aisle spaces were completely filled, converting the audience into a solid mass,—a proceeding which the fire laws of later days would not permit. When the services began there was scarcely a vacant foot of space throughout the entire interior.

Mr. Beecher had no manuscript—merely a few slips of paper in his hand. The pulpit was like an ordinary orchestral music stand—a mere shelf upon a single column. He stood beside, rather than behind it, and generally a considerable dis-

TWO FAMOUS PREACHERS

tance away from it, on a wide platform. At one crowded evening service when I was sitting next to the back row in one of the galleries, I was somewhat annoyed by a woman in a seat behind me who was leaning forward and thrusting her head over my shoulder. She was a plainly dressed woman, with a careworn countenance, well-advanced in life. I saw she was so completely wrapped up in what Mr. Beecher was saying that she was entirely unconscious of her position. He was preaching one of his most moving sermons on the burdens and trials of life, and when he finished and the vast audience sat in a hushed silence, I heard her say with a long sigh as she straightened up in her seat: "I can work another week now!"

I remember as clearly as if it were yesterday the ripple of amusement which passed over his great congregation one Sunday morning when, after a very eloquent passage, he paused a moment, and saying that his words were of personal, not general application, added:

The churches of the land are sprinkled all over with bald-headed old sinners whose hair has been worn off by the friction of countless sermons that have been aimed at them and have glanced off and hit the man in the pew behind.

NOTES AND ANECDOTES

That was a trying moment for the bald-headed men present, but it was a good example of the apparently unpremeditated outburst which he habitually employed and which served to hold keen and alert the attention of his hearers. There was never, so far as my observation went, any wandering of attention while he was talking, and no sign of somnolence.

I was speaking of his method once to an intimate friend of his who told me this anecdote which he vouched for as authentic. While on a sojourn in the country in summer Mr. Beecher attended the local church, sitting in the congregation. At the close of the service, the elders or deacons asked him to remain a few moments as they desired to consult him on a delicate question of church discipline. He tried to put them off, saying he had always refused to interfere in the affairs of another church than his own. They persisted, saying that it was a serious matter with them. Their congregation included a large element of farmers and other persons who worked hard during the week, and who, when they got into church on Sunday, were inclined to fall asleep, and, in some instances, to snore so loudly as to disturb the service. What could Mr. Beecher suggest as a method of discipline? He

TWO FAMOUS PREACHERS

replied with cheerful alacrity that a very effective remedy was in force in his church, and if they desired him to do so he would tell them what it was. They replied that that was precisely what they did desire. Whereupon he said:

"In our church we have had for some years an able-bodied committee whose duty it is, whenever any one is discovered asleep in the congregation, to go at once into the pulpit and wake up the pastor."

No less interesting than the regular Sunday services were the Friday evening prayer-meetings which were held in a large room attached to the church. At these Mr. Beecher sat in an arm-chair on an open platform and after reading a chapter from the Bible, talked in an easy, informal manner for a few minutes and then "threw the meeting open" for general remarks. On one evening when I was present a gentleman arose in the back part of the room and, with an air of one who should say: "Watch me now and see me put him a poser," said, as nearly as I can recall his words:

"Mr. Beecher, I come from the West (naming a town and state). We all read your printed sermons out there and we like them, but some of us have grave doubts about your orthodoxy.

NOTES AND ANECDOTES

With your permission I should like to state a hypothetical question and get your answer."

Mr. Beecher, with a cordial smile said: "I shall be very glad to hear it." The gentleman proceeded:

"I should like to suppose the case of a man who lives an upright and moral life; who is a faithful husband; a kind and generous father; a good citizen, taking part in all good works; gives freely to charity; in short, leads a life above reproach. Yet he is a pronounced disbeliever in Christianity, never goes to church, and is nothing less than an atheist. Now, Mr. Beecher, I should like to ask you: Where does that man go when he dies?"

Without changing his position, Mr. Beecher, with an engaging smile, replied: "He would have my best wishes, wherever he went."

On another occasion, after the meeting had been thrown open, a woman arose and entered upon a tiresome harangue on the rights of women —then a less absorbing topic than it became subsequently—lasting for half an hour. The audience evinced unmistakable signs of weariness, but Mr. Beecher sat calm and undisturbed. When she finished, he moved slightly in his chair and with a quiet smile said: "Nevertheless, brethren, I believe in women speaking in meeting."

TWO FAMOUS PREACHERS

The first time that I saw Mr. Beecher and Doctor Chapin pitted against each other was at a banquet of the National Publishers and Booksellers Association. It was a very large gathering composed of editors and publishers from all parts of the country. Doctor Chapin spoke first and made a most stirring address which showed marks of careful preparation. He had a voice of unusual volume, rich and sonorous, like the tone of an organ. He was an accomplished rhetorician and a master of eloquent sentences. His speech aroused great enthusiasm throughout and its closing passage brought the audience to its feet in a perfect uproar of cheers and waving napkins. I quote this passage as it was reported at the time:

"I love the rumbling of the steam-power press better than the rattle and roar of artillery. I like the click of the type in the composing-stick of the compositor better than the click of the musket in the hand of the soldier. It bears a leaden messenger of deadlier power, of sublimer force and of surer aim, which will hit its mark though it be a thousand years ahead."

Mr. Beecher was to come next. When the tumult subsided, and he arose, all eyes were turned upon him, and the general comment was: "Now we will see which of the two is the greater orator."

Beecher, with that knowledge of human nature which he possessed in so remarkable a degree, realized what was passing in the minds of the assemblage, and acted accordingly. With his hands clasped in front of him and in that wonderful voice of his—in tone quality remarkably like the voice of Joseph Jefferson, the actor—a voice whose lowest notes were plainly audible in the remotest corners of the room, he said very quietly:

"I know what my fate is on this occasion. After the profoundly eloquent remarks of the reverend brother who has just preceded me, what could I say that you would care to listen to? He has finished, but his resounding voice still fills this vast building, and in trying to say anything after him I am reminded of an experiment, which I once made when a boy, to ride behind two other boys, astride a lean, bare-backed horse. (Prolonged laughter.) I see you anticipate the result. I slipped off over the tail. I would not like to try that feat again with so many looking on as there would be here." He then spoke in a light, informal vein for ten or fifteen minutes, with no attempt at oratory.

I saw the two men pitted together again at the funeral of Horace Greeley in Doctor Chapin's church of which Mr. Greeley had been a member.

TWO FAMOUS PREACHERS

The church was packed in every part with those who had loved Mr. Greeley and whose hearts were sore with the grief which his tragic death had caused. Mr. Beecher was to speak first and Doctor Chapin was to follow. On a low platform in front of the pulpit a great mass of flowers was banked. Instead of ascending the pulpit Mr. Beecher took his stand among the flowers, and in his musical, low-pitched voice, without a gesture and without any display of oratory, spoke directly to the hearts of the assemblage, saying what every friend of Mr. Greeley longed to have said. After him Doctor Chapin from the pulpit delivered a scholarly oration, of marked intellectual merit, but not a sentence or a phrase of it reached a heart in his audience.

John Hay said of Beecher that he was "the greatest preacher that the world has known since St. Paul preached on Mars Hill." The secret of his greatness has always seemed to me to lie in his intense human sympathy. He preached the religion of humanity if ever man did.

CHAPTER V
JOHN HAY

ONE of the longest, most stimulating and helpful friendships of my life was that of more than thirty years with John Hay. When I entered the service of *The Tribune,* in December 1870, he was one of its editorial writers, having joined the staff a few weeks earlier. He was just back from an absence of five years in the American diplomatic service in Europe, two years as secretary of legation at Paris, one year as *chargé d'affaires* at Vienna, and two years as secretary of legation at Madrid. In each of these positions he had mastered the language of the country to which he was assigned and had acquired a thorough knowledge of its literature, art and institutions. How completely this was the case in regard to Spain, not only as concerned its language, literature and art, but its customs and traditions, stands revealed in his "Castilian Days," one of the most charming books in existence. He had enjoyed himself to the full in all these places and was fairly bubbling with delight over his experiences. A more joyful companion could not be imagined, for there was in him no trace of that melancholy which became almost habitual with him in his later years.

Only an echo of his charming personality came to the reporters over the screen which divided their room from that of the editors, but we all knew his editorials, for they were unlike any others in the paper. We had heard that Mr. Greeley had said that Hay was the most brilliant man who had ever entered the office and we agreed unanimously in that judgment. Our first question when we came together was: "Have you read Hay's article?" When in addition to his editorial contributions there appeared, in the early part of 1871, the first of the "Pike County Ballads," the immortal "Jim Bludso," the enthusiasm among us knew no bounds. We committed it to memory and recited it in part or in full on all possible occasions.

I was under the impression, till I examined the files of *The Tribune*, that the three best known of the "Pike County Ballads"—"Jim Bludso," "Little Breeches," and "The Mystery of Gilgal" —were all published first in the columns of that journal, but I find that the first-named was the only one that originally saw the light there. All were published together with the fourth, "Banty Tim," and other poems, by James R. Osgood in the spring of 1871, and were collected from various current periodicals. They had become as familiar as Bret Harte's "Heathen Chinee" by the time they appeared in book form, and were quoted almost as widely. Whether the dialect poems of Harte were the inspiration of the "Pike County Ballads" has been a more or less disputed question. The "Heathen Chinee" was first published in the *Overland Monthly* in August, 1870, under the title of "Plain Language from Truthful James. (Table Mountain, 1870.)" It was copied immediately in *The Tribune*, and, in fact, in every newspaper in the land. Hay's delight in it was unbounded, as had been his enthusiastic admiration for the "Luck of Roaring Camp" and the other stories with which Harte had leaped into fame. All the world, at least that part of it that had any connection with or interest in letters, went about talking of Harte and quoting him and reading him aloud when it assembled anywhere. The "Heathen Chinee" passed at once into the vocabulary and literary assets of every writer, from the most humble to the highest, and it was extremely rare to find a newspaper leader without a quotation from it, or to take part in a conversation in which reference to it was not made. Hay may have been influenced by his delight in it to compose his four dialect poems. They appeared, as I have shown, a few months later, and from the time of their publication were not infrequently confounded with the poems of Harte. The latter was often a visitor to *The Tribune* office in those days, and I have a vivid recollection of his description to Hay of an incident that had happened to himself at a literary reception on the previous evening, when a sentimental young woman assured him (Harte) that she had never read anything so delightful as his "Little Breeches," and that she really could not read it without laughter ending in tears.

Hay was always generous of praise for the work of others and depreciatory of his own. He was constantly saying of the poetry of the new school that arose after Harte in the West: "That is the real thing. They are doing what I would like to do and can't." He never for a moment ranked himself with Harte in speech, and I am sure he did not in thought. He spoke invariably of his "Ballads" as things of slight account, and by no means objects of pride. Many years after the time of which I am writing, an incident occurred which called forth from him an extremely

NOTES AND ANECDOTES

interesting letter about the origin of one of them. In December, 1888, a Mississippi steamer was burned under conditions strikingly similar to those described in "Jim Bludso." She caught fire, and her pilot headed her for the shore, jumping overboard when she reached it. The steamer was burning furiously and the lives of the passengers were in peril. She drifted away from the shore as soon as the pilot left the wheel. James Givens, a deck-hand, ran to the wheel, brought the steamer's head again to the bank, and in order to hold her there, locked the wheel in position. While he was doing this the flames completely surrounded the pilot-house. Givens, when his task was done, made a dash through the flames, jumped into the river, and struggled ashore, but died later of his injuries. He had literally "held her nozzle ag'in' the bank till the last galoot's ashore" in true Bludso fashion, and he saved seventy of the hundred lives on board.

When the accounts of the disaster were published here and abroad, the newspapers were quick to see the resemblance to the Bludso incident, and the ballad was reproduced far and wide. The London journals were especially interested in the coincidence, and made it the subject of a veritable renaissance of Hay literature. I made a collection of these utterances and sent them to Hay, with the result of receiving from him the following valuable and characteristic letter:

WASHINGTON, D. C., Jan. 11, '89.

MY DEAR BISHOP: I thank you very much for your kind letter and the inclosures, which I would not otherwise have seen. I thoroughly appreciate a good word for "Jim," who is a friend of mine. I shudder and hide in the cellar only when the Boy with the small knickerbockers is mentioned.

A curious thing happened during that summer when we were holding up the Republican party by the tail. [1881 when he was editor-in-chief.]

On the first appearance of "J. B.," Mark Twain wrote to me saying that I was all wrong making him an engineer—that only a pilot could have done what I represented him as doing. This troubled me somewhat—though I thought I was right. During the summer of '91, a cotton-broker of New Orleans, a son of "J. B." (whose name was Oliver Fairchild, by the way), came to see me at *The Tribune* office and absolutely confirmed my story, saying that his father *was* engineer of the *Fashion* and died in just that way. But my case was, of course, uncommon—the pilot usually does the work—and Jim Givens comes again to discredit me.

I am afraid this is ominous of my fate—to be right as a historian and wrong as an artist.

Wishing you and yours a happy New Year,
    I am faithfully yours,
        JOHN HAY.

NOTES AND ANECDOTES

After a service of about six months as a reporter and assistant city editor I was assigned to a subordinate position on the editorial staff and became an occupant of the main room which the editors shared in common. It was into this room that the intellectual visitors of whom I have spoken were in the habit of coming, and it was there that some of the best talk it has ever been my privilege to listen to was to be heard almost daily. It centred around Hay, who was always the leader and most delightful contributor, for he was the magnet that attracted the callers. My friendship with him began from the moment of my entry. He welcomed me with a cordiality so genuine and hearty as to win my heart for all time. And what a charmed circle it was into which to drop an impressionable youth to whom already the delights of the intellectual life seemed to be the highest given to mortals! Small wonder that his experiences therein were stamped indelibly upon his memory.

Hay wrote mainly upon foreign topics, political, social and literary, and always with the accent of intimate, personal knowledge. Into whatever he did, then and throughout his life, he put his full powers. He was preeminently a good workman; he would do nothing except his best.

But while he always did his best, he never made the mistake of taking journalistic work too seriously. He had the saving grace of humor, without which no journalist can hope to attain the largest measure of power and usefulness. I can best illustrate my meaning by relating an incident which occurred after he had been several years on *The Tribune.* It was the habit of editorial writers to spend the earlier part of the day in talk and to sit down to write in the afternoon. On this particular afternoon, toward evening, Hay came across the room to the desks of Bromley and myself, which stood side by side, and, displaying a handful of manuscript, said: "All done, fellows!"

"What have you written on?" I asked. Leaning over us and lowering his voice to a confidential whisper, he replied: "I've been going for them kings again, and *if they only knew it,* they'd be shaking in their boots at this moment."

He had small liking for journalism, great as were his talents for it, and was inflexibly determined to get out of it as soon as possible. He refused persistently to learn anything of the technical side of the business, saying whenever he was asked to do so: "I will not know anything of the kind. Nothing shall lure me into a permanent alliance with journalism. As some one has said of literature, it is a good mistress, but a wretched wife." He walked up to my desk, one night, between one and two o'clock in the morning, and urged me to go out to supper with the rest of them and then home. I said I could not because I had work that must be done. Looking at me for a moment, he said: "Bishop, I am sorry for you. You are a son of the Puritans, and a victim of that curious disease called conscientiousness." You had to know John Hay in order not to misunderstand that remark. A more conscientious man never lived, but his saving sense of humor forbade that his conscientiousness should ever become a disease.

At another time, when we were speaking of a common acquaintance who had suddenly reversed his attitude toward a question of large public importance and was advocating his new view with an astonishing air of conviction, I said that I could not understand him at all, for I was quite sure he had been influenced by interested motives. "Of course you cannot understand him," said Hay. "You have a Puritan conscience, and there is no arguing with that; but he has a conscience that is far less troublesome, for it permits him to believe whatever he wishes to." He had an unerring insight into character, and a sure and always light touch in pointing out its salient quality. It was not till you had thought for a moment of what he had said that you realized how much there was in his half-humorous and seemingly careless utterance. The quickness of his humor was equal to its lightness. I could give many instances of this in his *Tribune* experience, but one must suffice. One night, when the whole force was on duty late, news came of the death of an illustrious personage whose obituary must be prepared in haste. Noah Brooks, who was usually called upon for such emergencies because of his readiness as a writer, went to the library for books and returned with an armful, moving in a peculiar jog-trot gait that he adopted when in a hurry. As he passed Hay's desk, the latter, without looking up or pausing in his writing, said as if merely thinking aloud: " 'Books in the running Brooks.' "

Hay remained with *The Tribune* as an editorial writer for about five years, leaving it in 1875. He returned as temporary editor-in-chief, in April, 1881, at the request of Whitelaw Reid, during the latter's absence on his honeymoon. The two men had been close friends for many years and the political course of *The Tribune*, as well as its

NOTES AND ANECDOTES

general policy, had been shaped so completely by them that it might with truth be said they were its joint editors. Hay took charge in the midst of the factional fight which Senator Roscoe Conkling, of New York, was making on President Garfield. The attitude of *The Tribune* in that fight was defined clearly before Reid's departure and Hay was in full knowledge of it and in full accord with it. In view of these unquestionable facts, the following statements about Hay's editorship, in William R. Thayer's "Life" of him, are curiously inaccurate: "He (Hay) could not be sure that he was running *The Tribune* in each crisis as Whitelaw Reid would have done, and therefore he wisely concluded to run it as seemed best to himself." There was nothing on earth that Hay was more "sure" of than Reid's wishes in a crisis and he followed the fixed policy of the paper without variation or shadow of change. Even if he had not been in complete accord with Reid's ideas, Hay would have been quite incapable of the disloyalty of reversing or altering the paper's policy while acting as a *locum tenens* for its chief.

To every member of the editorial staff, Hay's six months' occupation of the chair of editor-in-chief was a period of constant delight. He was the ideal director and guide—always keenly appreciative and inspiring, and always holding control with a firm, sure hand. His ability to "hold his rudder true" was put to the test when in July, 1881, President Garfield was assassinated. The news of that reached New York about ten o'clock in the morning and aroused an outburst of horror and indignation which has rarely been equalled. Immense crowds began to gather immediately in front of the newspaper offices, awaiting anxiously the latest news from Washington. All through the day they stood there in complete silence, for the bulletins from the sick bed gave little or no ground for hope. When evening came the crowds reached proportions which were limited only by the capacity of the streets. The newspaper offices, at that time, were all situated in Printing House Square and along Park Row. These and City Hall Park were packed with a dense throng that occupied every foot of space. Viewed from the upper stories of *The Tribune* building, the scene was the most moving and impressive I have ever beheld. I had seen the same space filled on election nights, but with a far different throng—a mass of men shouting, cheering and singing campaign songs. What I saw on that evening was a great sea of faces, deadly pale under the glaring electric light, all lifted toward the high-hung bulletin board, and all stern and tense in a silence that no voice disturbed. Far into the night this silent mass remained, and when, near midnight, a bulletin was posted, reading: "The President has rallied and there is hope," the silence was broken with an outburst that was not so much a shout of joy as a huge sigh of relief from thousands of overstrained hearts. Not till then did the crowds slowly melt away.

Within *The Tribune* office during the evening there gathered a considerable assemblage of indignant and enraged Republicans, partisans of the stricken President, who sought to convince Hay that he should charge responsibility for the crime upon those who had precipitated the party quarrel. One of these actually contended that the title of *The Tribune's* editorial article on the assault should be "Roscoe Conkling—Assassin!" There were many other suggestions scarcely less wild. Hay, who had remained perfectly calm amid the storm, with no sign of hesitation or doubt as to what course he should pursue, let the excited gentlemen have their full say, listening to all with an expression of quiet interest. When they had finished he showed them so clearly, in a few quiet words, both the folly and danger of their counsel, that they went away convinced and somewhat ashamed. I was present throughout the scene, being in council with Hay at the time, and it seemed to me that he managed the situation much as Lincoln would have done, for his long and intimate association with Lincoln had made him familiar with his methods. He showed on this occasion, as he showed repeatedly in the trying days which followed during the long illness of Garfield, the essential quality of a great editor,— ability to keep his head in a crisis.

Constant association with Hay during the six months of his editorship placed our friendship on an enduring basis. After he entered public life we were always in close touch with each other, either through frequent personal intercourse, or letters, which were nearly the same thing, for his letters were like his talk. He could not talk in a dull or uninteresting way, neither could be write a dull letter. Unlike many brilliant letter-writers, he did not write with the obvious expectation of subsequent publication. He let himself go freely, as was his wont in familiar conversation, and the consequence was that he never wrote without saying something that the recipient of the letter would most unwillingly let die. I have had many such letters from him which, to my vast regret, I destroyed.

NOTES AND ANECDOTES

I was talking with him one day in Washington while he was Secretary of State, when he spoke of the extraordinary number of letters that Gladstone had preserved, and said that they should be of incalculable value to the historian, adding the words about the value of such letters which I have quoted in the first chapter of this book. "Why," I exclaimed, "you have written me dozens which you have enjoined me to destroy as soon as read, letting no eye but mine see them, and I have obeyed you, though it took all my moral strength to do so." He waved my protest aside with a laugh, but I shall never cease to regret that I was not in possession five years earlier of his views about the value of such letters. In the early part of 1901 I wrote to him at the State Department, asking him to tell me in strict confidence what he thought was likely to be the outcome of a threatened disturbance in a South American country. "It is difficult to say," he replied, "what will happen on the Spanish Main. It is the land of the fantastic and the unexpected." In the midst of the Presidential campaign of 1904, the curious discovery was made and published that the chairman of the Democratic National Committee had the same name as one of the principal characters in "The Mystery of Gilgal." The

JOHN HAY

scene of that ballad is laid in "Taggart's Hall—Tom Taggart's of Gilgal," and one of the stanzas is:

"Tom Taggart stood behind his bar,
The time was fall, the skies was far.
The neighbors round the counter drawed,
And ca'mly drinked and jawed."

I sent a paper containing the reproduced ballad to Hay, and in replying, he wrote: "Thanks for your letter and the paper. I thought of that coincidence the other day, and wondered whether I should escape. It was a curious case of innocent prophecy."

The sudden death of his eldest son in the summer of 1901 was a blow from which he never recovered. It deepened and made permanent that shadow of melancholy that, during his later years, had been lurking about him. I waited for some time before writing to him, in order to separate myself from the great flood of condolence that I knew would pour in upon him from all parts of the world, and received a reply really tragic in its pathos:

Newbury, N. H., Aug. 30, 1901.

My dear Bishop: I thank you for your kind letter. I have received many like it—and have answered very few. I think of little else when I am not at work, and

NOTES AND ANECDOTES

even when I am busy his genial, powerful face, with its winning smile, is continually coming before me, his rich mellow voice and jolly laugh are sounding in my ears. To think of all that splendid vitality, that abounding force—to which almost any achievement would have been easy—extinguished at dawn, and I, like Browning's waning moon, "going dispiritedly, glad to finish."

I could not get away from my post—everybody agreed—and for a little while longer I suppose I am as well there as anywhere. I have been working all summer—to good purpose—and shall have several important bits of work to submit to the Senate, if nothing adverse happens. But after that—no one can tell . . . I am not sanguine, though leading Senators assure me it will be all right this time. At least my course was clear; I had to try again, to save us from a threatened dishonor. If I fail again, I shall know what my duty to myself requires.

Yours faithfully,
JOHN HAY.

I have heard many good talkers in my time, thank God, but none better than John Hay. His conversation was literally a "joy forever." It was that and more. There was in it an intellectual exhilaration that was contagious and irresistible. He loved to talk and his keen joy in it was so genuine and so obvious that it infected his listeners. He was as good a listener as he was a talker, never monopolizing the conversation at table or elsewhere, never "taking the floor," and never treating the company, as Queen Victoria said Mr. Gladstone treated her, like "a public meeting." He talked without the slightest sign of effort or premeditation, said his good things as if he owed their inspiration to the listener, and never exhibited a shadow of consciousness of his own brilliancy. His manner toward the conversation of others was the most winning form of compliment conceivable. Every person who spent a half-hour or more with him was sure to go away, not only charmed with Hay, but uncommonly well pleased with himself. Surely, he reflected, as he passed out of that enchanted circle—surely there must be something above the ordinary in my own thought and conversation, since Hay can find such obvious pleasure in them. Hay once said to me of Mr. Evarts, of whose gifts as a conversationalist we were speaking, that he had the rare faculty of saying at a dinner-table the best thing that was said there,—invariably something that was quoted everywhere for days and even years afterward,—and giving the impression while saying it that he had better things in reserve if he really cared to produce them. Hay possessed much the same faculty. Surely he never left upon any one the impression that he had exhausted his intellectual resources.

It was simply impossible for him to talk for any length of time without saying something that delighted you inexpressibly, and that you could carry away and tell to others for their delight. I was talking with him on one occasion, while he was Secretary of State, about some negotiations that he was conducting with two of the "most fantastic and unexpected" of the countries of the Spanish Main. After telling me of his efforts to reach an agreement with the special envoys who had been sent to Washington for the purpose, there came into his eye that inimitable twinkle of enjoyment which was always the herald of a coming good thing, and leaning forward in order to get into a more thoroughly confidential position with me, he said: "Talking with those fellows down there, Bishop, is like holding a squirrel in your lap and trying to keep up the conversation."

Not long after Roosevelt acceded to the Presidency, an amiable but somewhat self-laudatory gentleman who found much pleasure in appointing himself to important diplomatic missions returned to Washington from a brief trip abroad and went about saying he had been to England on a secret mission of great moment for the President and the Secretary of State. In an unlucky hour he said this in the hearing of a newspaper correspondent who published it. Our friend, whom we will call Jones for the moment, was then in an extremely embarrassing position, from which he endeavored to extricate himself without delay. I happened to be in Washington about a week later, and in the course of a talk with Hay I said: "That was a very amusing incident about Jones and his 'secret mission.'" To this Hay replied: "I am grateful to Jones, for he gave me the opportunity of saying the one good thing I have said in my life. I usually think of them too late, but this I thought of in time. I knew, when I read about Jones's 'mission' in the morning paper, that he would call at the State Department before the day was far advanced. His card came in very soon after I reached the office, and I had him shown in at once. Stepping up to my desk in visible trepidation, he began to deliver a little speech which he had obviously prepared with care. 'Mr. Secretary,' he said, 'I sincerely trust that nothing that I have done in this matter has in any manner embarrassed you in your negotiations with Great Britain, and I think I can say with entire truth that I have done nothing for which I should blush.'

"When he paused," said Hay, "I realized that the Lord had delivered him into my hands, and with all the suavity I could command, I said: 'Mr. Jones, I can assure you, without the slightest reservation, that nothing that you have done has in any manner embarrassed me in my negotiations with Great Britain, and I can assure you, also without reservation, that I am quite sure you have done nothing for which you could blush.'"

"Did he see it?" I asked. "Certainly not," replied Hay. "He went about Washington, saying he had just come from a most satisfactory interview with the Secretary of State." "Had he any authority?" I asked. "Jones—authority? Why, Bishop, I am amazed at your ignorance. Jones is viceregent of the Almighty in all international affairs!"

One morning in Hay's house on Lafayette Square in Washington, when President Roosevelt and William H. Taft, who was then Secretary of War, were present, the latter said:

"I see that the anti-imperialists are changing their ground about the Philippines. They have been saying heretofore that we should not have stayed there after the battle of Manila; that we should get out of them and leave them to their fate; and that they are doing infinite harm to us and to our institutions, because in ruling them against their will we are violating the Declaration of Independence and destroying our own love of liberty. Now they say that we ought to give them away, or sell them to Germany or Japan or any nation that will take them off our hands." "That," said Hay, "reminds me of the young woman who had got religion and was telling her experience in conference meeting. Wishing to give proof of the thoroughness of her conversion, she said: 'When I found that my jewelry was dragging me down to hell, I gave it all to my sister.'"

He was assailed venomously and offensively for several years by a man in public life for no apparent reason except a personal grudge. When news of this man's death reached Hay he said: "I believe thoroughly in *De mortuis nil nisi bonum*, but he was a low down skunk and I'm glad he is dead!"

We were speaking one day about the pertinacity of office-seekers. "I will tell you," said Hay, "an incident that has never been published about Lincoln. I was sitting with him on one occasion when a man who had been calling on him almost daily for weeks in pursuit of an office was shown in. He made his usual request, when Lincoln said: 'It is of no use, my friend. You had better go home. I am not going to give you that place.' At this the man became enraged, and in a very insolent tone exclaimed, 'Then, as I understand it, Mr. President, you refuse to do me justice.' At this, Lincoln's patience, which was as near the infinite as anything that I have ever known, gave

NOTES AND ANECDOTES

way. He looked at the man steadily for a half-minute or more, then slowly began to lift his long figure from its slouching position in the chair. He rose without haste, went over to where the man was sitting, took him by the coat-collar, carried him bodily to the door, threw him in a heap outside, closed the door, and returned to his chair. The man picked himself up, opened the door, and cried, 'I want my papers!' Lincoln took a package of papers from the table, went to the door and threw them out, again closed it, and returned to his chair. He said not a word, then or afterward, about the incident." There have been many pictures of Lincoln, but few more graphic than that, as Hay drew it for me.

It was hard for those who knew and loved Hay—and all who knew him did love him—to reconcile themselves when he was taken from us to the thought that he could draw no more pictures for us; that this admirable and perfect and rarely matched artist in words could delight us no more forever. As he said of the voice of his son, his own is still sounding in our ears.

President Roosevelt, speaking at the Harvard Commencement in 1902, said: "It is a liberal education in high-minded statesmanship to sit at the same council table with John Hay." It was a

JOHN HAY

liberal education in the delights of the intellectual life, the highest gift that Heaven has bestowed upon mortals, to sit in intimate companionship with John Hay and watch the play of that well-stored and brilliant mind. No one who had enjoyed that supreme privilege could ever forget it—forget the musical voice, which in every tone and fibre was the voice of the intellectual man; the clear-cut enunciation; the unerring use of the right word and the only right word in every instance; the wide knowledge of men and nations, of peoples and governments; the familiar and every-ready knowledge of all that is best in literature, and over it all the play of a humor which was next-door neighbor to melancholy and all the finer for that close association.

Never after his death was I able to pass beneath the windows of his library in that beautiful Washington home where I experienced the highest intellectual pleasure I have ever known, without saying to myself, as a sense of supreme and irreparable loss sank deep into my heart:

> "O for the touch of a vanish'd hand,
> And the sound of a voice that is still!"

CHAPTER VI

ISAAC H. BROMLEY—WILLIAM WINTER

ONE of the most joyful—using the word in the sense of diffusing joy around him—men that it has been my good fortune to know was Isaac H. Bromley, universally known in the State of Connecticut and in the wider realm of anecdote and reminiscence as "Ike" Bromley. One could scarcely cross the border line of Connecticut in his time, and for many years after, without encountering an anecdote, invariably a delightful one, of him or of his doings. He was for many years an editor in that State, and his name was a familiar one in every corner of it, always mentioned with a smile and the narration of a "good thing" he had said. His was that happy humor which seldom left a sting. The victim of it enjoyed it as much as anybody else, unless he had provoked it in some way that deserved punishment. In such case, he invariably "got what was coming to him."

My acquaintance with him began when, after

I. H. BROMLEY — WILLIAM WINTER

Horace Greeley's death, he joined the editorial staff of *The Tribune* early in 1873. His advent in the office was a distinct novelty, for it was the entry of an individuality of a kind never before employed on the paper. In fact, he was the kind of writer who would be a novelty on any newspaper into whose service he might enter. He was the possessor of a written style that was solely his own. Nobody else ever wrote like him, and his editorial articles were never mistaken for those of any one else. His appearance as a contributor to the editorial page fairly startled the older members of the staff. When his first contribution was put in type, the sensation created in the office was upheaving. Asked if he did not think the article was funny, one of these elder heads replied: "It may be funny, but it is not half so funny as the idea of publishing it on the editorial page of *The Tribune* is!"

In the eyes of this veteran, such publication amounted to sacrilege, for it flew in the face of all the most sacred "traditions of the paper," and there is nothing at once so immovable and so deadly in a newspaper office as the "traditions of the paper." Left undisturbed long enough, they will accomplish the decay and death of the most powerful journal on earth. Gustave Le Bon says:

"There is nothing so destructive as the dust of dead gods." There is nothing so destructive to a newspaper as the dust of a dead tradition.

Bromley's appearance in *The Tribune's* editorial page was undoubtedly a rude shock to tradition, but it was an instant and unbounded joy to the readers of the paper. They hailed it with delight, and the news of the arrival spread rapidly over the land through the columns of other newspapers which hastened to reproduce his contributions.

I shall attempt no description of Bromley's style, leaving the citations, which I shall make presently, to speak on that point. Underlying all that he wrote was a keen sense of humor which was peculiarly that of New England—the humor of the Yankee in his pristine estate. It detects with infallible certainty the flavor of humbug in an individual or an utterance and pierces it with unerring precision. As William Winter, his associate on *The Tribune,* said of Bromley in a graceful tribute at the time of his death:

> "His was the keen, satiric touch
> That shrivels falsehood into dust."

Both in speech and in writing, Bromley maintained invariably an outward demeanor of serious-

I. H. BROMLEY — WILLIAM WINTER

ness. He never smiled while saying the most amusing things, never laughed at his own jokes, being in that respect like Mark Twain, who preserved inflexibly an aspect of unutterable woe throughout a narrative that was convulsing his auditors.

To illustrate Bromley's quick perception of affectation or humbug, I will cite a few instances which came within my personal attention and which rise up in my memory as I write. It was his habit to sit in silence most of the time near groups where others were talking, carefully noting all that was said. On one occasion in *The Tribune* office, a member of the staff was seeking to impress with his knowledge of old books a visitor who was known to be a collector of rare volumes. "Speaking of old books," he said, "there's Bayle's Dictionary. If I were shut up in prison and allowed only one book, I should take Bayle." Instantly, without even a twinkle of the eye, Bromley, as if in surprise, said, "Why you could get out with that!" On another occasion I walked into a club café with him, and as we entered a gentleman visibly under alcoholic inspiration, who was addressing a group on the opposite side of the room, cried: "There's Brom. Hullo, Brom, come over here. I have been telling these gentlemen the terms of a bet I have made, and I want your opinion on a disputed point. I have bet that if Blaine is renominated (this was in 1888) he will carry every Northwestern State. Now the question has arisen what States are implied in the term Northwestern." Promptly and quietly came the reply from Bromley: "Well, the state of intoxication is implied in the terms of the bet."

One evening he entered *The Tribune* office and coming to my desk said: "There is a distinguished visitor from Rhode Island up at the Fifth Avenue Hotel." "Who is he?" "The Ambrosial Burnside." "What is he doing there?" "Walking up and down the lobby, shrinking from the public gaze." Any one who was familiar with the martial bearing, dangerously approximating a strut, and the famous whiskers of General Ambrose E. Burnside, will recognize the graphic accuracy of that description.

Travelling on a Sound steamer one evening, a pompous gentleman, obviously engaged in "shrinking from the public gaze," pervaded the vessel. Bromley rushed up to him, shook him heartily by the hand, asked how he was, how his wife and children were, and expressed great joy at sight of him. The pompous person responded with some embarrassment, and, after answering all Bromley's questions as to the health of his family, said: "But you have the advantage of me—" "Oh, no," broke in Bromley. "You never saw me before, did you?" "No," was the reply. "Well, I never saw you before."

"What was your class in college?" I asked him one day. "Well," he replied, "my class was 1853, but I did not stay till the end. In the Junior year the Faculty called on me in a body and suggested that as I was so far ahead of the rest of the class I had better stop out and let them catch up."

At a class banquet, Edmund Clarence Stedman, a classmate of Bromley, gave a batch of reminiscences of the latter's exploits in the university. When he had finished Bromley was called upon and said: "I am not a poet, like Stedman. I have had no dealings with the muse; but if I ever feel like touching the lyre and I am anywhere near Stedman I'll put my hand right on his shoulder."

Mr. Congdon, the veteran member of *The Tribune* staff whom I have cited in a previous chapter, developed a keen interest in theology in his later years and was fond of discussing it on all occasions in the editorial room. On one of these, when Bromley and I, seated side by side, were deeply engaged in writing what Bromley was wont to call "beautiful thoughts for to-morrow's paper," Congdon began pacing up and down behind us, dilating on his favorite topic. Pausing for a moment by Bromley's chair he said earnestly: "What we want, what we must have, is a larger idea of the nature of the Deity." Turning his head over his shoulder, Bromley exclaimed: "Advertise, advertise!"

One of Bromley's first editorial articles to attract wide attention was on an incident which had occurred in Washington. Caleb Cushing had made complaint in police court that he was annoyed beyond endurance by the barking of a dog which belonged to Fernando Wood, his next-door neighbor. Under the title of "Cave Canem," Bromley opened his article as follows:*

"Five hundred dogs in this town," remarked Mr. Elias Cottrell as he contemplated from the curbstone a canine procession that was slowly developing into a wild tangle of abstract dog—"five hundred dogs," said he in his slowly deliberate style as if putting down his first stake for a problem in political economy and getting ready for a grapple with statistics; and then he added in the weary way with which one is apt to announce the discovery of

*Tribune, July 19, 1873.

I. H. BROMLEY — WILLIAM WINTER

some new social maladjustment—"and I suppose two hundred and fifty would do all the business."

After a discussion of the various kinds of dogs the article proceeded:

Mr. Caleb Cushing is a man of the most varied acquirements. Familiar with all the modern languages, he reads with the greatest ease the Sanskrit and the Syriac, converses fluently in Hebrew and Greek, and speaks Chinese like a native. To him the inscriptions on the tea-chest and the fire-cracker are plain as a pikestaff, and Confucius in the original no mystery. His next-door neighbor in Washington is Mr. Fernando Wood—or rather, to be more exact, Mr. Fernando Wood's yellow dog. Mr. Fernando Wood's yellow dog seems to be a sort of night-blooming Serius with a Peruvian bark—and his bark was on the C. C. To Mr. Caleb Cushing, whiling away an hour or two at midnight with the Targum or some light Childaic romance, Mr. Fernando Wood's yellow dog in the adjoining yard, stirred thereunto by some remorseful memory, put forth his mouth and lifted up a wail. It startled the rapt scholar like the cry of a Congressman who dreams that his back pay has lapsed. . . . To the scholarly mind at midnight even the transient serenade of the bibulous has its exasperations. What then must have been the effect upon the eminent philologist of the midnight latrations of Fernando Wood's yellow dog? Picture the sage at his open window with the raised boot-jack, forgetting the affluence of his resources in all languages living and dead, addressing Fernando Wood's yellow dog in the simple energetic eloquence of the profane! Here was Cushing—there was the dog—heights and distances and a door-yard fence intervened, and though boots and boot-jacks, and the folios of a statesman's library, and frequent sulphurous ejaculations filled all the ambient air, the aim of the great publicist had not improved with age, and the dog, lying perdue, howled on.

His most successful article, and the one longest remembered, was that entitled "Logan on His Feet." It was carried about in pocketbooks and pasted in innumerable scrapbooks to my personal knowledge. I can quote only parts of it but the entire column of it well deserves reproduction:

Pranced there in upon the arena of the great debate, like a trick mule in a circus, or a spavined nightmare on the track of a beautiful dream, Logan of Illinois. There was a vision of mustaches, eyebrows, and hair piled on each other in arches, a large brandishing of arms, a pose, and a stridulous war-whoop, and much as though a picture of the Deerfield massacre had stepped out from the pages of history, Logan took the American Senate by its large, capacious ear. And then he went for his mother tongue. He smote it right and left, hip and thigh, and showed no mercy. Swinging the broadaxe of his logic high in air, he turned it ere it fell and with the hammer side struck the language of sixty millions of people fairly in the face and mashed it beyond recognition. . . . He shut his teeth into the language as the untamed tiger of the jungle takes between his mouth and paw the wear-

I. H. BROMLEY — WILLIAM WINTER

ing apparel of the wayfarer and the ripping of it was heard through all the forest depths. . . . So through two hours Logan swung his beautiful arms over the heads of the Senate, like the booms of a government derrick, while his chin churned the language like a pile-driver in a heavy sea, and the baffled reporters made wild plunges with their pencils to gather up his regurgitations for the printer.

Whatever may be said of this style of editorial writing, no one can deny that it was and is unique in journalism. Nothing like it had appeared before his time or has appeared since. He imitated nobody and nobody has imitated him. It had the supreme quality of readableness, for no one could begin the perusal of one of his articles without finishing it—and the prime essential of newspaper writing is that it shall be read.

Yet great as was Bromley's success as an editorial writer, his most wide-spread triumph was achieved by a bit of doggerel which was published with no suspicion of its nearly unlimited possibilities of popularity. In the summer of 1875 one of the street-car lines in New York City posted the following notice in its cars:

The conductor, when he receives a fare, will punch, in the presence of the passenger,
A blue trip-slip for an eight-cent fare,

A buff trip-slip for a six-cent fare,
A pink trip-slip for a three-cent fare.

This had been posted for several weeks and had attracted no attention as containing lyrical qualities. Sitting in one of the cars on an evening journey down-town with his friend, Noah Brooks, formerly of *The Tribune* staff but then on the staff of *The Times,* Bromley said suddenly; "It's poetry, by George! Brooks, it's poetry!" Brooks, who had been dozing, asked what was poetry. Pointing to the notice Bromley said: "Why, don't you see? The lines are all of the same length and all begin with a capital letter. Doesn't that make poetry?" Reaching *The Tribune* office, he wrote out the "poetry" as follows:

"The conductor when he receives a fare,
  Will punch in the presence of the passinjare,
  A blue trip-slip for an eight-cent fare,
  A buff trip-slip for a six-cent fare,
  A pink trip-slip for a three-cent fare,
  All in the presence of the passinjare."
Chorus: "Punch, brothers, punch with care," &c.

In the work of composing, Bromley was aided by members of *The Tribune* staff but the inspiration was all his own. The "poem" was published inconspicuously on one of the inside pages of *The*

I. H. BROMLEY — WILLIAM WINTER

Tribune, without signature, but its merits were so extraordinary that it could not remain hidden. It was copied instantly by newspapers in all parts of the country. It not only caught the popular fancy but seized upon it like a nightmare. Once fixed in the memory, it stayed there in spite of all efforts to be rid of it. In my journeys in the cars where the notice was displayed, I saw passenger after passenger get in, seat himself, and as soon as his eys fell upon the notice, he would begin mumbling, as his lips showed, the tantalizing lines. From that moment, he was doomed. He could only take his eyes away by leaving the car. I saw a serene Quaker couple, in the beautiful garb of their faith, fall captive in this way. They sat down opposite the notice, and their eyes fell upon it simultaneously. With a slight start, they looked inquiringly at each other, then back to the notice, and then the mumbling of the lips began.

Everybody fell a victim to the jingle. It was set to music, parodied, and quoted everywhere and on all occasions. Mark Twain caught the infection and wrote an amusing account of his sufferings which was published in the *Atlantic Monthly,* in February, 1876, under the title of "A Literary Nightmare," in which he maintained that the only way by which he could rid himself

NOTES AND ANECDOTES

of it was to give it to somebody else. This publication gave rise to a quite general belief that Mark Twain was himself the author of it, and that belief persists to the present day. In *Scribner's Monthly*, of April, 1876, Bromley himself, under the fictitious name of "Winkelried Wolfgang Brown," published a true account of the authorship, claiming for himself the honor of founding a new school of verse to be known for all time as "Horse-car Poetry."

Its fame spread to other lands and it was translated into other tongues. *The Western*, a St. Louis magazine, found relief in a Latin anthem, with the chorus,

> "Pungite, fratres, pungite,
> Pungite cum amore,
> Pungite pro victore
> Diligentissime pungite."

It reached Paris and appeared as follows in the *Revue des Deux Mondes*:[*]

LE CHANT DU CONDUCTEUR

Ayant été payé, le conducteur
Percera en pleine vue du voyageur,
Quand il reçoit trois sous un coupon vert,

[*] See Albert Bigelow Paine's "Biography of Mark Twain," Vol. I, p. 557.

I. H. BROMLEY — WILLIAM WINTER

Un coupon jaune pour six sous c'est l'affaire.
Et pour huit sous un coupon couleur
De rose, en pleine vue du voyageur.

Choeur.

Donc, percez soigneusement, mes frères,
Tout en pleine vue des voyageurs, &c.

Cheerful, joy-diffusing soul was Bromley! His mere presence in a newspaper office was worth a liberal salary, for he kept alive and alert at all times that saving grace of humor which is the newspaper's most valuable asset. His quick and unerring perception of the ridiculous side of a subject, or of the humbug in it, of a pose in advocacy of it, held at safe distance the peril of being too serious which hangs over every really earnest and conservative journal. His constitutional inability to remain serious for any considerable length of time prompted him to sudden and surprising deliverances which acted as an intellectual tonic upon any conversation in which he was a participant. I recall a particularly characteristic instance of this which occurred one evening in the café of a prominent New York club. A group of men had been talking together for an hour or more, the conversation growing steadily more serious under the influence of successive libations until it had reached finally the great mystery of life and death. As quite often happens, such is the curious effect of alcohol upon some temperaments, the more bibulous members of the party were the most solemn contributors to the discussion. Bromley had listened, without saying much, until the time of departure arrived. Then, with great seriousness and deliberation, he said: "Well, there is one great principle that underlies it all and explains it all; but I don't recall it at this moment, and I don't give a damn!"

Another member of *The Tribune* staff of those days, admired and loved by all his associates, was William Winter—poet, essayist, critic and charming gentleman. For forty years he was the dramatic critic of *The Tribune* and during that entire period he was the undisputed head of the profession in the United States. He wrote with the authority of a student who was thoroughly versed in the history, tradition and literature of the stage and in a style which it was an intellectual delight to read, for he was the facile master of a remarkably wide and rich vocabulary and wrote English with extraordinary skill. The same intellectual charm distinguished his many poems and his books of travel and of the stage and life. In both poems and books there is a pervading air

I. H. BROMLEY — WILLIAM WINTER

of gentle melancholy. The poems are always graceful, musical, perfect in form, for he had the soul and the inspiration of a genuine poet, but they are almost invariably sad. He wrote many elegiac verses in memory of actors and others who had been his friends, and they were among the best he ever produced, for in this form of utterance his muse found its finest and fullest expression.

It might be said of him that as life advanced melancholy became more and more a habit. He was a delicate and sensitive creature and the "vile blows and buffets of the world" were hard for him to bear. It was said of him by one who knew him well, that he ought to have lived in England in the time of Queen Anne and been granted a pension by the Queen. Not only did melancholy become a habit, but one could fancy him saying at times with Samuel Rogers:

> "There's such a charm in melancholy,
> I would not, if I could, be gay."

On one occasion, when he was especially deep in gloom, Bromley remarked to me as he left us: "Billy is very mouldy to-day; he is in the graveyard again."

Walking up to my desk one afternoon when I

was absorbed in writing, he held out in the palm of his hand beneath my eyes a small watch, its case richly studded with jewels, and in solemn tones said: "That watch was sent to me by Adelaide Neilson. It reached me simultaneously with the news of her death. 'Twas as though she had said: 'Take it. I have done with time.'" In this instance, as in many others, the effect of his long and intimate association with the theatre was revealed in his speech. He had become theatric in expression quite unconsciously.

He was, as I have intimated, a past-master of the use of language. On occasion he could put a wealth of meaning into a few words or even a single word. He had a thorough detestation for the mawkish plays of the Ibsen-Sudermann school. I sat with him through one of them, and as it ended I asked him what he thought of it. "Putrid!" was the reply. I was with him again when Beerbohm Tree gave his melodramatic performance of Hamlet, with the spotlight following him about the stage even in the ghost scene where its presence was enough to startle even the ghost. When at the close Hamlet, dying in the full glare of the spot-light, said: "The rest is silence," Winter ejaculated: "Thank God!"

With his tendency to melancholy Winter had a

I. H. BROMLEY — WILLIAM WINTER

fund of dry humor and was unusually quick-witted. At a public banquet at which he was one of the formal list of speakers, General W. T. Sherman was the presiding officer. The general was then advanced in years and was clearly unfamiliar with the duties of the position. He became confused with the list of toasts and called up Winter to speak upon one which belonged to some one else. Winter arose with a quizzical smile and began his speech by saying: "The mistake which our honored chairman has made in the subject of my remarks places me in an embarrassment like that which befell a darky preacher whose custom it was to open the Bible at random, read the chapter that his eye first fell upon, and use it as the text of his sermon. In one instance he opened it at a chapter in Genesis in which the progeny of Adam was set forth with the names of the persons whom each descendant had begat. The preacher read it laboriously through, pronouncing the word "forgot" in each case. When he had finished he paused in deep thought for a moment and then said: 'All dis goes to show, brederen, dat dem old patriarchs was mighty fergitful.' "

He craved sympathy and during our many years of unbroken and affectionate friendship we

NOTES AND ANECDOTES

spent many hours in intimate converse which usually ended in his taking a more cheerful view of things simply by the arousing of his sense of humor. A year after I resigned from *The Tribune* to accept a position as editorial writer on *The Evening Post*, I received a letter from him which is so characteristic of the gentle nature of the man that I venture to append it here:

NEW BRIGHTON, S. I., June 19, 1884.

MY DEAR BISHOP: You have often shown a kind feeling toward me, and often endeavored to do me good. I am wishful you should know that I appreciate your kindness, and certainly I do not wish to fade out of your memory. I have ordered three of my books to be sent to you, from Boston—my "Poems," "The Trip" and "The English Rambles." The packet was to be sent to you at the office of *The Evening Post,* and would be marked "Personal." Will you be so kind as to let me know whether it has come. I am always, truly your friend

WILLIAM WINTER.

J. B. BISHOP, Esq.

CHAPTER VII

EDWIN L. GODKIN

IN August, 1883, at the personal invitation of Edwin L. Godkin, Editor-in-Chief of *The Evening Post,* I joined the staff of that journal as an editorial writer. From that date till near the close of the year 1899 I retained that position and during the intervening period my relations with Mr. Godkin were so continuously agreeable that I look back upon those sixteen years of close association with him as the most enjoyable and profitable of my journalistic career of thirty-five years. It was literally a liberal education in thinking as well as in writing to be with him. He granted me a degree of intimate companionship which he accorded to few men. It was not easy for him to be confidential with anybody. Direct and open he always was, sometimes to an extent well-nigh terrifying; but confidential, in the sense of disclosing to you his inmost feeling as well as thought, he seldom was with anybody. He detested sentimentalism in every form, and had an infallible scent for it, no matter in what guise it might approach him. In his eyes it was a form of humbug, and that was enough to condemn it. I have never come in personal contact with a mind so free from cant as his was. He did not need Dr. Johnson's injunction, "First clear your mind of cant," for the taint had never entered his. He had that perfect intellectual sanity and perfect intellectual integrity which stand revealed in the works of Huxley and Darwin, and more clearly still in the private letters of the two. What they sought, Mr. Godkin always sought with a zeal and determination that nothing could resist—the thought at the bottom of every question which carried conviction with it. He was intensely eager to get the honest thought of other men, but the thought that he held to finally was the one that carried conviction to his own intellect. When he had decided upon that, it became the law and the gospel for him, and there was no power on earth capable of swerving him from his devotion to it. Other men might call him intolerant; he knew to the very depths of his soul that he was right.

I can most clearly reveal the qualities of his mind by citing some illustrations of his methods. It was his custom to hold each morning an informal conference of editorial writers upon the subjects which were to be treated in the day's paper. At this conference it was understood that everybody should "free his mind" without restraint, and this was always done. What was especially calculated to unnerve a newcomer in these gatherings was the intensity of concentration in Mr. Godkin's eyes, when he turned to him, after the latter had proposed a subject, and asked: "What would you say about it?" Woe to the poor man if he had nothing above the commonplace view to present. He would not get far in his exposition before, with an impatient wave of the hand, and whirling quickly around in his chair, the chief would dispose of the matter with an unceremonious verdict, like, "I don't think that's worth while," or, "We have said that already," or, "Oh, there's nothing in that." After that, nothing more upon the subject was to be said. Sometimes, after an interested attention of a few seconds, a quick, searching question would be put that would go through the subject like a knife through a toy balloon, leaving complete and utter collapse. But if a real thought were brought forward, an old subject with a novel method of treatment advanced, Mr. Godkin's eye would kindle with delight, his mind would at once begin to play around it, illuminating it with touches of humor and expanding it with penetrating insight, till the author became fairly astonished at the beautiful proportions of his own offspring. Just at this point came the author's greatest peril. The chances were ten to the dozen that Mr. Godkin would become so delighted with the development of the subject, so intoxicated with the intellectual pleasure of its treatment, that he would say, with a serene smile of perfect enjoyment: "I'll write on that."

But the loss of his subject was not the worst misfortune that happened to the subordinate editor. He was destined to see it treated in a manner that might well fill him with despair. Not only was all that he thought about it expressed in a way that he could never hope to equal, but with it a veritable host of ideas that had been lurking in his mind, but which he could not get hold of. It was this quality in Mr. Godkin's writing that Lowell defined so exactly in one of his letters to him: "You always say what I would have said—if I had only thought of it." And how well he said it!—with an inexhaustible supply of quiet, delicious humor, and a wealth of experience and knowledge. Everything was grist for his mill. A casual quip in conversation, the latest good story, a sentence from a new book, a fresh bit of political

EDWIN L. GODKIN

slang—all these found lodgment in his mind, and just at the proper place they would appear in his writing. Time and time again I said something to him that I thought would interest him, and failed to get the least response, or even a sign that he really comprehended it; yet, as certain as fate, it would stare me in the face a day or a week later, fitting into a leading article as nothing else would have fitted in that place, and as I myself would never have had the thought of using it.

He was as ready to listen to criticism of a subject of his own proposing as he was to assail a subject advanced by others. All he asked of you was perfect frankness and sincerity and the possession of a real thought. If you had something to say that was worth saying, a more eager listener or a more responsive one could not be desired. If you got the better of him, and showed him a defect in his own idea, he did not hesitate for a second, after he had argued the point with you, to admit defeat. So, too, with his work after it appeared in "proof." Any suggestion of change that was made and was of value he would take instantly. He had less of the vanity of authorship than any other man I have ever known. Delight in his work he always took, but it was from sheer enjoyment in the intellectual exercise at-

NOTES AND ANECDOTES

tending it—an enjoyment which seemed as detached from himself as if it were the work of another person. He had in very large measure the faculty of walking around himself, looking at himself at a distance and from all sides, which was of incalculable value in his work. Many a time when he thought of writing upon some topic that needed careful treatment, I have heard him say: "I want to write on it, but I don't know whether I can trust my discretion." He was always on the watch for his rollicking humor, lest it lead him into extremes of expression that might prove harmful to the cause he was striving to aid. Time and again he would write something, and before putting it in type take counsel on it, watching you closely to see if you caught the humor of it and comprehended fully what he had said in it. If you failed in this test, he would never ask your judgment again. If you met the test, but advised against publication, backing your advice with good reasons, he would suppress the matter without a particle of hesitation or compunction, and say no more about it.

Nothing delighted him more than what he was fond of calling "journalistic rows." When one of these broke out between two or more contemporaries, he always followed it with intense en-

EDWIN L. GODKIN

joyment, and sooner or later fairly itched to take a hand in it. The "joy of combat," inherent in the Irish blood, was strong in him, and he knew he must watch it. Repeatedly, when a "row" was on, he would write something about it, just by way of trial, and then take advice. If you said in criticism that in writing about it he had committed some of the most flagrant of the offenses that he had for years been assailing as the leading characteristics of these "rows," he would burst into a roar of laughter and say: "Well, I am afraid that is so, but I really should like to show what a pair of humbugs they are." But he would destroy his "copy" nevertheless. Never was his enjoyment of a "row" keener than when he himself was the object of attack, as was very often the case. He would read all the hard things said of him in one paper after another, fairly shaking with pleasure, and then say: "What a delightful lot they are! We must stir them up again." If the able editors who thought they were making him miserable with their "scathing" attacks upon him as "Larry" Godkin could have seen him under these conditions, they would have been greatly astonished.

The secret of his unusual conduct under fire was given with entire accuracy by Mr. E. C. Stedman, to whom I was once describing it. It was his consciousness of power. "He knew that he could hit back much harder than they had struck." And he could. No assailant who ever fell under his editorial hand would deny that. I was once asked to go to a friend, a man of high character and unusual influence upon the intellectual life of his time, who sent word to me that he was ill in bed. I found him in bed, really ill, and the cause was that he had been made the subject of Mr. Godkin's powers of ridicule for something he had done which offered provocation for that treatment. "I do not care a rap," he said, "for what any other editor may say about me, but Mr. Godkin has the awful power to wound." When I told Mr. Godkin of this, he was quite overcome with contrition, and said, with perfect sincerity, that he had no idea the man would take it so hard as that. "I will never write another word about him," he added, and he never did.

His unfailing sense of humor kept his mind in a condition of perpetual youth. Although in years he was the oldest man on his staff, intellectually he was the youngest member of it. His ability to take fresh views of an old subject, to find in it a phase that gave it new interest, was inexhaustible. No man was ever less prone to get into ruts. His objection, always ready to a suggested topic, "Oh, we've said that," was a constant prod to research and original thought. At the same time he was a firm believer in the gospel of iteration, and when any kind of campaign of education was in progress, he insisted upon enforcing it; but even then he was always able to give each succeeding application a sufficient touch of variety to make it attractive. When he was conducting his memorable assault upon the personnel of the old Republican machine of New York City, he hit first upon the device of always referring to its members as the Boys, with a capital B, and this from the moment of its appearance in print became the established usage. Then followed his repeated designation of them as the "Johnnies," "Jakes," and "Mikes," with quotation-marks, and the use of all names of other Boys in like manner. A peculiarly characteristic touch came later, when, in speaking of their political work, he described them as "engaged in their Jakery and Mikery." There were people who complained of weariness because of his persistence in the use of this nomenclature, but it was undoubtedly most effective in bringing that kind of political activity into disrepute.

He had the ability, somewhat rare among men of humor, to appreciate a joke when he was him-

NOTES AND ANECDOTES

self the victim of it. When he first took editorial charge of *The Evening Post* he had associated with him two other well-known Mugwumps, Carl Schurz and Horace White. The combination did not work harmoniously, and after a year or more Mr. Schurz withdrew. There was much speculation in the newspapers as to the cause of the disagreement, and the suggestion was made by Isaac H. Bromley of *The Tribune,* that "there were too many mules in the same pasture." Mr. Godkin was inexpressibly tickled with this, and always recalled it with hearty laughter. On one occasion a gentleman who had been appointed to public office was spoken of in a sketch of his life which was published in the local columns of the paper as "the son of an Irishman living in Alabama." He came into the office in a condition of great wrath and insisted upon seeing Mr. Godkin personally about it. He saw him, and after he had departed Mr. Godkin came out of his room with his face fairly beaming with amusement and said: "Don't you think there is something comic in a man's coming to *me* with the claim that he has been insulted by being called the 'son of an Irishman'?" On another occasion a well-meaning but very unsophisticated reformer came to me with a wonderful tale of great things

EDWIN L. GODKIN

he and his associates were doing in municipal politics. When I failed to be sufficiently impressed with the value of his labors, he asked, as a personal favor, to be introduced to Mr. Godkin. I presented him and retired. Within a few minutes he fairly burst from Mr. Godkin's room, his face aflame and his gait very rapid. Behind him, a minute later, came Mr. Godkin, his eyes flashing and his whole countenance emitting wrath. Striding up to my desk, he exclaimed: "There is only one answer to be made to the stuff that man talks, and that is, 'You're an ass!'" "Did you make it?" I asked. "No," he replied; "but I came very near doing so." "I judge from his appearance as he departed," I said, "that he was able to gather your meaning, nevertheless." Then the humorous aspect of the case struck him, and his wrath disappeared in a hearty laugh.

No matter how earnest or how indignant he might be about anything, the moment a ludicrous view of it appeared, he was ready to enjoy it, not infrequently to the sacrifice of all other aspects of it. One thing he would not submit to, and that was to be bored. The city during the height of his career was fairly crowded with persons who had made this discovery under circumstances far from agreeable to themselves. If a stentorian yawn, or a deep sigh, would not start a bore, heroic methods were resorted to so effectively that an active enemy for life was usually made. I was complaining to him one day that a person to whom he had introduced me was boring me almost beyond endurance. "Why don't you let him see it?" he asked. "I do," I replied, "in all the usual ways, but he refuses to recognize them." "Then I would ask him to please go away," he said. "I have always found that effective."

He was amused always with that perennial type of reader known to all publishers as the "stop-the-paper" subscriber. Whenever he received an angry letter from one of them, his invariable form of reply was that the letter furnished indubitable evidence that the writer stood in especial need of the enlightenment and instruction which the paper was supplying, and that hence it would be sent to him for the full period of his subscription. On one occasion he received a long and extremely pretentious communication from a "constant reader," criticizing his conduct of the paper and instructing him at great length and with much specification as to the way in which he should edit it. Mr. Godkin replied with studied courtesy, saying that he had read the letter with much interest and was deeply impressed with the writer's desire to aid him in editing the paper. Still, he felt obliged to say that he was convinced that the writer was laboring under a misapprehension as to the value of his own opinions. If those opinions, he added, were as valuable as the writer evidently believed them to be, the house in which he lived would be surrounded with large hotels that would be crowded with pilgrims from all quarters of the earth who had come there to get the benefit of his advice. The fact that his dwelling was not so surrounded should convince him that he was putting too high an estimate upon his views. Nothing further was heard from this critic. Few critics, in fact, ever ventured upon a second encounter.

From the outset of his career as editor the charge of "omniscience" was brought against him. Charles Dudley Warner struck a chord of approval in many hearts when he dubbed *The Nation*, when Mr. Godkin was editing it in its early days, "The Weekly Judgment Day." Undoubtedly Mr. Godkin had always with him the conviction that he was right—what man of really strong intellect has not? In almost every case he was right, or, to put it in another way, he was more nearly right than his critics. He was better informed than they were, had a profounder knowledge of the subjects he was discussing, and brought to them more careful thought than they could command. The reasons for this were to be found in his intellectual training and experience. I do not think it will be disputed that he was the best and most widely educated man who has entered journalism in this country. As a "great editor" he stands in a class by himself. No one would think of placing him in the same category with Greeley or Bennett or Raymond or Dana. As a purely intellectual man he ranked above them all. He was the son of an eminent scholar, and was born into as well as trained for the intellectual life. He entered American journalism on its intellectual side and remained on that side throughout his career. All his interest in his newspaper centred in the editorial page; he paid only casual and superficial attention to the other parts of it. Then, too, he was from first to last the philosophic observer of events, viewing them in this country more or less as an outsider. In times of unusual excitement he was capable of becoming an insider for the moment, but he invariably resumed his attitude of observer subsequently.

In commenting upon American politics and development he was always weighing them in the light of human history, with which he had the familiarity which came from constant reading

EDWIN L. GODKIN

and intimate personal knowledge of the leading minds of his time. From the time when, as a young man just entering upon life, he wrote a history of Hungary, down through the period when he went as a newspaper correspondent to the Crimean War, and till his later days, he lived in constant association with men and books. He was as familiar with every phase of European politics as he was with those of this country, his knowledge coming not only from books, periodicals, and newspapers, but from personal acquaintance, resumed almost yearly in long visits abroad, with the leading statesmen and publicists of nearly every country in Europe. No other American journalist possessed such advantages as these, and he was naturally aware of the superior power which they gave him.

And was he the only editor who has assumed greater wisdom than his fellows? Lowell, writing to him in 1867, said: " 'Tis the curse of an editor that he must always be right. Ah, when I'm once out of the *North American Review* won't I kick up my heels and be as ignorant as I please! But beware of omniscience. There is death in *that* pot, however it may be with others. It excites jealously to begin with." Note the rare insight of that final sentence, and you will find, I think, a partial explanation of the attitude of many of Mr. Godkin's esteemed contemporaries toward him. He not only assumed to be always right: in most cases he was right. Few things are harder to bear in a fellow-being, especially in a fellow-editor, than a steady-going quality of that sort.

But while he was intolerant of ignorant or superficial criticism, he was never so toward men in whose sincerity and intelligence he had confidence. *The Evening Post,* under his editorship, was the home of that absolute intellectual freedom, intellectual courage, and intellectual honesty without which there can be no great newspaper. Every subject was discussed in the editorial council with a freedom of opinion that was simply unlimited. When the paper spoke, it uttered the combined view of the entire staff as it had been arrived at in the discussion. Sometimes, probably in a great majority of instances, the original view of Mr. Godkin was the one expressed, but often he had abandoned that for a different one brought forward by some one else. He had no pride of opinion, but, on the contrary, hailed with positive delight one that he recognized as superior to his own. He would fight for his own for all it was worth until convinced, and would fight at times with a good deal of human heat; but when the tussle was ended, even in his own defeat, there was not a trace of bitterness or injured vanity. Nothing was more intolerable to him than the modern conception of the intellectual side of a newspaper,—the conception that has come in with the advent of commercial journalism,—which looks upon the editorial page as the mere tender of the business side, its writers as so many hands in a factory, rather than as constituting the soul of the paper.

Was he a pessimist, had he no faith in American institutions, was he never an American in feeling and sympathy? I have left these questions till the last, because they call for the most careful treatment, and because I am aware that a large number of people will not agree with what I shall say about them. When I first became associated with him, on the eve of the Presidential campaign of 1884, he was an optimist, in the proper sense of that much-abused word. He detested dishonesty and trickery in political and public life, but he scorned the idea that these were dominating influences, or that the American people were indifferent to them. He threw himself into the task of preventing Mr. Blaine's election with all his force and with an unshakable conviction of ultimate success. I remember distinctly that, as the campaign drew to a close and the virulence of partisan bitterness reached a degree of intensity rarely if ever known in this country, before or since, he never for a moment faltered in his faith as to the success of his view of the case at the polls. On the day of election, when we were all weary with the long and bitter contest, and when, as is inevitable in such a condition of overwrought nervous tension, many of us were troubled with anxious doubt as to the result, he was imperturbably calm. When I expressed my fear on the subject, he said, with an earnestness of conviction that I shall never forget: "I have been sitting here for twenty years and more, placing faith in the American people, and they have never gone back on me yet, and I do not believe they will now." That was his invariable spirit in all the early years of my association with him. It was still his spirit in 1888, for when Lowell delivered his address in this city, in April of that year, on "The Place of the Independent in Politics," Mr. Godkin, in commenting upon it on the following day, said:

What was better than all was that there ran through every sentence a vein of that high morality and courageous hopefulness, and of that supreme confidence that, in the long run, the better cause will have the upper hand,

EDWIN L. GODKIN

which, to men who are worth much either to home or country, always sounds like a trumpet blast. Every one who listened to him, and, above all, those who have to deal with the unspeakable meannesses and trivialities of factional politics, must have been grateful for being raised for one brief hour into the pure air and the clear light which surround the things that ought to be.

The key-note of all his labor at that time and for several years afterward was "courageous hopefulness." He believed in his work, and believed that " in the long run the better cause will have the upper hand." He never could understand the persistent criticism of his methods that he was a destructionist, that he tore down rather than built up. Time and again he quoted, as expressing his creed, Lowell's familiar lines:

"I loved my country so as only they
Who love a mother fit to die for may,
I loved her old renown, her stainless fame;
What better proof than that I loathed her shame?"

He believed with all his mind and heart that there was no surer way to bring about better politics, higher standards of political morality and conduct, than by merciless exposure of political wrongdoing, and merciless condemnation of those who were responsible for it. On one occasion, when a somewhat timid reformer was remonstrating with him for what he regarded as too great resort to personalities, he exclaimed: "My dear sir, rascals in all ages have objected to personalities!" He believed in denouncing sinners, rather than sin. His conception of his duty as a journalist was much like that which Socrates in his 'Apology' said his had been in Athens: "The state is exactly like a high-bred steed, which is sluggish by reason of his very size, and so needs a gadfly to wake him up. And as such a gadfly does God seem to have fastened me upon the state."

With all his zeal and persistence, he believed in times and seasons for reform work, and had little patience with the type of reformer who could not see that there were times for action and times for inaction. In fact, from the outset of his career as a journalist, he was shy of the "crank" reformer. He had constant trouble with his early abolitionist associates, because he could not discard entirely the saving quality of common sense in his editorial course. Many of them parted company with him early in his career, and others were unable to approve his conduct or to keep faith in him. He was always on his guard against too close identification with them in the public eye. His sense of the ridiculous was so acute that he feared the consequences of attaching that quality to any cause he was advocating. Many times did I hear him say in the presence of such danger: "We must keep those people in the background as much as possible, or we shall become ridiculous."

His whole soul revolted at the war with Spain. He once told me that the sight of a battle-field in the Crimea, after the fight was over, had given him a loathing for war that he could not overcome, no matter what the provocation might be. As to the Spanish War, he believed it to be unnecessary and unjust, and that it could have been prevented and would have been prevented had not Congress precipitated it. When it came, he was unable to reconcile himself to it, and he remained in this attitude to the end. He did not believe that the institutions of the country could survive it without a radical change in character, and when the people of the country sustained both the war and the administration under which it had been fought, he was convinced that the character of the American people also had changed. His old buoyant faith that "in the long run the better cause will have the upper hand" was dead within him, and he saw nothing but the breakdown of free institutions in America as the ultimate and not far-distant outcome. There is no reason why

NOTES AND ANECDOTES

I should not speak freely of this attitude of his. He made no concealment of it, for it was not possible for him to conceal what he believed to be the truth. Hour after hour would he argue a point with me, with much of the old intellectual vigor, but without a ray of the old hopefulness. He had simply given up the fight, and having given it up, saw nothing but gloom in the future. Time and again he would exclaim, when I refused to accept his view: "I cannot see how you keep up your optimism!" On one occasion when we had found ourselves getting further and further apart, he went away, but returning a few minutes later, said with that directness which was his distinguishing characteristic and noblest attribute: "I am going to ask you a direct question, and I want a direct answer. Do you think age is telling on me?" When the direct answer was given that in some ways it was and in others it was not, and that it showed most in a growing unwillingness to hear the other side, and in despair of the future because his advice had not been followed, he answered with great simplicity, that old quality of walking around himself for an impartial view still unimpaired: "Well, you know, I am very near the border-line."

It was impossible after this period to arouse the

EDWIN L. GODKIN

old hopeful spirit by any appeal whatever, even to his sense of humor. In the earlier days he would always be ready to laugh over a charge that he was a pessimist. "Why," he would say, "they have been calling me that for forty years. When I lived in Cambridge, and spent much time with Charles Eliot Norton, they used to say that, when Norton and I sat up late at night discussing political men and affairs, about two in the morning things became so dismal that all the dogs in Cambridge began to howl."

If he was a pessimist, he was the most cheerful as well as the most delightful one the world, or at least my part of it, has ever known. If ever there was a life of intellectual freedom, it was the life which had him for its centre and moving spirit. We hear a great deal nowadays about restrictions upon intellectual freedom, and several persons who claim to have had theirs restricted have filled the land with clamor about their sufferings. Mr. Godkin had the first requisite of intellectual freedom, an intellect to be free with, and that he used it for the welfare of his fellow men no one can successfully dispute. He did, for nearly a quarter of a century, perform that inestimable service that Lowell attributed to him of "heightening and purifying the tone of our political thought." He made journalism in this country an intellectual profession to which any man of talent might be proud to belong, and for this all journalists owe him a debt of lasting gratitude.

CHAPTER VIII

THEODORE ROOSEVELT

AS I look back over the quarter of a century of my intimate friendship with Theodore Roosevelt it seems to me that the quality in him which dominated all others was his humanness. He was the eternal human. Lord Morley, English essayist and biographer of the first rank, said of him after a visit of several days to him when he was President, that in him the country had "got a man." Later he said of him: "He is not an American, you know. He is America." That is the Roosevelt I knew—not only a man but a man who was the living embodiment of the highest aspirations of his country. With the keen, dispassionate eye of a trained analyst of men and character, Lord Morley had reached a judgment which every intimate and associate of Roosevelt recognized as profoundly wise and profoundly true.

It is in accordance with this view of Roosevelt that I shall venture to record here some of my personal recollections of him. I shall endeavor to exhibit him as a man, not as a superman; as a thoroughly human being, not a demigod. They do him a poor service and one that would call forth his wrath did he know of it, who strive to picture him otherwise. He could say with Abou Ben Adhem: "Write me as one who loves his fellow men." But he loved them with discrimination. He could hate as well as love. Perhaps I should say detest rather than hate, for there was a total lack of vindictiveness in his nature. He could denounce a man savagely and a few months later show a kindly feeling toward him. His anger was fierce but it soon burned itself out. There was in him nothing of the Indian who never forgets and never forgives. He might remember for years, but forgiveness was easy and seldom long delayed. Toward certain specimens of his fellow men his detestation, freely expressed, was never abated. Foremost among them stood the persons whom he branded permanently as "Mollycoddles," men "who think feebly and act feebly"; and "Pacifists" whom he regarded as enemies of their country. Toward others, like those whom he included in the "Lunatic Fringe of Reform" he had only a mild and amused contempt. "Give me a wise serpent to work with rather than a harmless dove," he often said.

His general attitude toward his fellow men was

hospitable. He greeted them with an open mind and was ready to trust them if they showed themselves worthy of trust. His inclination, which remained with him, only slighty shaken, till the end of his life, was to take at their word all persons who came to him with professions of devotion to the principles for which he stood. He put faith in them till indisputable proof of their unworthiness came to him, and then he turned away from them for all time. They had no second chance. Soon after he became President of the Board of Police Commissioners in New York an instance of this kind arose. One of the commissioners was a tricky and unscrupulous politician who set himself at work from the start to thwart Roosevelt's efforts for reform. He covered his designs with fervid professions of devotion to Roosevelt, and completely duped him. I warned Roosevelt against him but to no purpose; he simply replied that while the man might have been tricky in the past he was convinced of his entire loyalty to him. He was not long in finding out his mistake. I was upholding in *The Evening Post* of which at the time I was an assistant editor, Roosevelt's course in the Police Department. The wily commissioner sought to make trouble between Roosevelt and me. He asked me to stop Roosevelt talking so much for the newspapers, saying it was injuring their work. I laughed and said: "Stop Roosevelt talking? Why, you would kill him. He has to talk. The peculiarity about him is that he has what is essentially a boy's mind. What he thinks he says at once, thinks aloud. It is his distinguishing characteristic, and I don't know as he will ever outgrow it. But with it he has great qualities which make him an invaluable public servant—inflexible honesty, absolute fearlessness, and devotion to good government which amounts to religion. Furthermore, he is talking for a purpose. He wishes the public to know what the Police Board is doing so that it will have popular support."

It was at this stage of his plot, in his ignorance of Roosevelt's character, that the commissioner, in the picturesque language of Uncle Remus, "drap he wattermillion." He went to Roosevelt with a perverted account of what I had said, little thinking that Roosevelt, with that straightforwardness which was a distinguishing characteristic, would go at once to me, as he did. He asked me by telephone to lunch with him. As soon as we were seated at a narrow table he leaned forward, bringing his face close to mine, and with appalling directness said: "Parker came into my office this morning and said: 'You think Bishop is a friend of yours, don't you?' 'Yes,' I replied. 'Well, you know what he said about you last night? He said you had a boy's mind and it might never be developed.'"

Roosevelt's eye-glasses were within three inches of my face and his eyes were looking straight into mine. Knowing my man, I did not flinch. "Roosevelt, I did say that. Did he tell you what else I said?" "No, that is what I want to hear." When I had told him, he brought his fist down on the table with a bang, exclaiming: "By George, I knew it!" He made no objection to what I had said about his mind, but that he had noted it I discovered several years later, when he was the Republican candidate for Vice-President. He had returned from a speaking tour in the West and I complimented him upon one of his speeches, saying frankly that it was a better speech than I thought he could make. With a roguish grin he said: "My boy's mind is developing, eh!"

This incident established our friendship so firmly that nothing was able to disturb it. He detested backbiting of all kinds, and always suspected the motives of the man who employed it against a friend of his. He gave his confidence wholly and was the most loyal of friends, but he never made a mess of friendship. There never was a man more entirely free of sentimentalism of all kinds. The mere suspicion of it gave him intellectual nausea. Of a friend he asked the same frankness and honesty in intercourse that he practised himself. If he asked for an opinion on some act or thought of his own, he desired only that it should be an honest one. "What I value in you," he said more than once to me, "is that you give me the advice you think I need rather than the advice you think I'd like to have." He was hospitable to criticism but inhospitable to flattery. It could not be said of him as was said of quite a different statesman: "He is not the sort of man who lies awake nights watching his limitations." He saw his limitations both day and night. "Mind you," he said to me many times, "I have not a particle of genius. I have certain abilities and I use them for all they are worth, and that is all." On one occasion when he had asked me to spend the night at Oyster Bay, he met me at the door with a smile, saying: "I have done a mean thing to you. I have written twelve speeches which I am going to make on my Western tour and I'm going to read them to you and ask you for suggestions." When he began to read one, and looking up caught an unconscious smile on my face, he said: "What are you smiling at?" I had learned never to dodge a query of that sort from him. "Why," I replied, "I have heard you say that so many times that I could repeat it backwards myself." "Of course," he said, "I know that; I know I have said it and I know it is full of platitudes. I am not an orator. I can't talk anything but platitudes. But platitudes and iteration are necessary in order to hammer the truths and principles I advocate into people's heads. Every elementary truth and every platitude or axiom ought to be repeated publicly not only every day but every hour for the good of the nation."

One of the most familiar jocosities of "Tom" Reed, of Maine, was uttered soon after Roosevelt became President: "Roosevelt has discovered the Ten Commandments and is tickled to death with them." This was a jibe on its author's part, but it was also a confession of his own attitude toward the Ten Commandments. He had used the word discovery in a secondary sense, and not in its first and full meaning which is to "uncover," "to lay open to view," or "to make visible." Roosevelt perceived that the country stood in need of having the Ten Commandments called to its attention and he proceeded to uncover them and to keep them in full sight for many years.

NOTES AND ANECDOTES

He may not have had genius in his own conception of the word, but one element of genius he surely had and that is the quality or gift of foresight. He could see further ahead in the march of events than most men of his time. Only with regard to his own fortunes was this gift denied him. At every stage of his public career he believed that the end of it had come. Shortly before he retired from the Police Department he said to me: "This is the last office I shall ever hold. I have offended so many powerful interests and so many powerful politicians that no political preferment in future will be possible for me. All the liquor interests, including the great breweries, and all the party bosses will oppose me, and no political party will venture to defy an opposition so fatal as that is. I realized this when I began my fight for the enforcement of the Sunday law and against police bribery and corruption, but it was the only course I could honestly pursue and I am willing to abide by the consequences."

When, in spite of his efforts to prevent it, he was nominated for the Vice-Presidency and elected, he said to me: "I am neither disappointed nor depressed, though I look upon it as the end of my political career. I have been Governor of New York and held other important public offices;

THEODORE ROOSEVELT

I have won a modest amount of military honor, and can leave to my children the record of a career of which they will not be ashamed. If I have been put on the shelf, my enemies will find that I can make it a cheerful place of abode. For occupation I shall resume the study of the law, get admitted to the bar and begin active practice of the profession."

When next I saw him he was in the White House as President. On his way from Buffalo, after taking the oath of office there, to attend the funeral of President McKinley in Canton, he sent a telegram to me to come to him at the White House on the evening of his arrival there, Sept. 20, 1901. He was alone in the house when I arrived, for his family had not yet come, and there was no other guest present. We had a long and intimate conversation in which he talked freely of his policies and purposes as President. I said to him that no man had ever entered upon the office more absolutely free than he was of all obligation to anybody; that he owed his possession of it to no one, but that, on the contrary, he had acceded to it in spite of persistent efforts of his most zealous enemies to prevent him from ever reaching it; and that he would enter upon his duties with the certainty of holding the office

NOTES AND ANECDOTES

for seven and a half years. He replied at once, and with great emphasis:

"I don't know anything about seven years. But this I do know—I am going to be President for three years, and I am going to do my utmost to give the country a good President during that period. I am going to be full President, and I rather be full President for three and a half years than half a President for seven and a half years. Now, mind you, I am no second Grover Cleveland. I admire certain of his qualities, but I have no intention of doing with the Republican party what he did with the Democratic party. I intend to work with my party and to make it strong by making it worthy of popular support."

He repeated this declaration in similar terms to Sir George Otto Trevelyan, the eminent English historian, in a letter which he wrote to him on May 28, 1904, and which I quote in order that I may cite the comment which Sir George made upon it. Roosevelt wrote:

"I certainly would not be willing to hold the Presidency at the cost of failing to do the things which make the real reason why I care to hold it at all. I had much rather be a real President for three years and a half than a figurehead for seven years and a half."

THEODORE ROOSEVELT

Commenting on this, Trevelyan wrote to me April 23, 1919, when I was engaged in writing Roosevelt's *Life*: "What wisdom is in this letter, and what courage! If there is a finer and truer description of a statesman's creed extant in the world, I do not know it."

That he was a real President during the period in which he held the office no one can deny. He was on the job every minute, was always master of it, and was always purely Rooseveltian in his methods and conduct—that is, unlike any President who had preceded him or any President who was to come after him. Henry Adams said of him that he was "pure act." He was; and he took profound joy in action. How did he like being President, he was asked, and the quick reply was: "I am having a bully time!" It was no less a joy for an intimate observer to watch him in action, or to have him talk about it, for he was an irrepressible and illimitable talker. His mind was so full that it overflowed in speech at every opportunity. His critics said of him that he talked so much that no one else had a chance to get in a word and that conversation when he was present was simply a monologue. It must be admitted that this was apt to be the case, but even his critics acknowledged that the monologue was interesting.

NOTES AND ANECDOTES

The effect of his flood of conversation, so lacking in formality and so limitless in volume, was especially overpowering when turned upon foreign visitors. I was a fellow guest in the White House when John Morley, afterwards Lord Morley, made a visit of several days to the President in November, 1904. We arrived together on the second day after the national election in which Roosevelt had been chosen President by the votes of the people. He was fairly bubbling over with joy because of his great triumph and was talking, not merely thirteen to the dozen, but fully one hundred and forty-four. The effect upon Mr. Morley, a cold, deliberate, slow-speaking and formal Englishman, was almost dumbfounding. He was scarcely able to get in a word, and was obviously experiencing difficulty in keeping pace with the mental processes of his host. Early in the evening he pleaded fatigue and retired to his room. When we met the next morning he asked me how long the President and I had talked after he left us, and when I said an hour or more, he drew a deep breath and exclaimed: "He's a most extraordinary man!" Later in the day, after more conversation with the President, he placed his hand on my shoulder when we were alone and said: "My dear fellow, do you know the two most

THEODORE ROOSEVELT

extraordinary things I have seen in your country? Niagara Falls and the President of the United States—both great wonders of nature!" This remark hugely delighted Secretary Hay and Secretary Taft when I repeated it to them, and it did not displease Roosevelt when I told him of it. That Mr. Morley did not use the expression in a disparaging sense he showed a few days later when, in the course of a conversation which he and I were holding on French history, he said in speaking of Napoleon: "This man whose guests we are has many of Napoleon's qualities—indomitable courage, tireless perseverance, great capacity for leadership—and one thing that Napoleon never had—high moral purpose! And think what it would have meant for the world if he had had that!" I quote from memory and am not sure of the exact phraseology, but the sense is as I have expressed it.

It was the physical vigor of the President which Mr. Morley had in mind in his Niagara Falls remark. A frail man himself, in delicate health, the sight of the exuberant vitality of Roosevelt fairly wearied him. After a dinner one evening, during which the President had been in buoyant humor and had done much of the talking, he was taking leave of his guests whom he had followed into the hall talking and gesticulating in his usual emphatic manner. Mr. Morley touched me on the arm, pointed to him and said: "Look at him! And he has been doing that all day long!" As he said this he sank into a chair as if completely exhausted by the mere sight of such tireless energy.

In September, 1905, at the personal request of President Roosevelt, I was appointed Secretary of the Panama Canal Commission, a position which I held for nine years, extending not only through his presidential term but through the entire period of canal construction. The first two years of my service I spent in Washington and the remaining seven on the Isthmus, resigning from the service in June, 1914, when the canal had been completed and thrown open to traffic. During my two years in Washington I was in constant communication with the President and had unusual opportunity to study his official methods and conduct. My personal relations with him had been so intimate for several years that I was apprehensive lest I should forget at times our official relations and be unduly familiar. I said as much to him and in reply he scoffed at the idea but added: "On one point you must be on your guard. Your personal relations with me are well known and politicians and others who are always on the watch for hints about my purposes and plans will take note of anything you may say in that direction. You will have to be very discreet when they are about. As for me, I am so perpetually indiscreet that nobody pays the slightest attention to me." I thought of that many times subsequently when his frankness of speech on social and semi-social occasions fairly astounded me, but though outbursts of this kind were frequent and occurred in the presence of considerable numbers of people, and, if made public, might have done him serious political harm, his confidence was rarely or never betrayed.

While I was on duty in Washington there was a virtually continuous assault upon me by the politicians who had been stirred to wrath because I, having no political standing and no political following, had been given an office which they regarded as part of their legitimate spoils. When I spoke of this to the President, he said: "What you want is a good coat of pachyderm. They are not aiming at you but are firing at me over your head!" "Yes," I said, "but they are hitting my head."

In the height of this assault there congregated in my office one afternoon a group of newspaper correspondents who fell into a conversation about members of both houses of Congress, relating many anecdotes and incidents concerning them which were far from complimentary. I interposed soon after this talk began, saying they were in a Government office and that I, as a Government official, ought not to allow it to go on. They pooh-poohed the idea, saying that we were all newspaper men, I having been one myself, and that it was all confidential. A few days later, to my consternation, I found a column or more, in the form of a Washington despatch, in the New York *Herald,* headed: "The Kind of Man Bishop Is," and in this all the various stories told by the assembled correspondents, not one of which had been contributed by me, were put in my mouth. I started at once for the Executive Office, and finding the President disengaged was shown at once into his presence. White and trembling, I asked him if he had seen the article. "What is it?" he replied. I told him, saying that I had said none of the things attributed to me, but that I knew at the time that I ought not to have allowed them to be said and that in failing to stop the conversation I had shown myself unfit to hold public office. Seizing the paper by one corner, he swung it in the air, flung it on the floor, and exclaimed: "Well, by George, all the fault I have to find with you is that you pay the slightest attention to anything that appears in the New York *Herald!*"

A few days later *The Herald* correspondent came to the door of my office and asked if he could come in. I replied that if he could stand it I could, whereupon he said: "You can't blame a man for doing what I did if he has to do it or lose his job, can you?" He went on to say: "Mr. Bennett cabled from Paris to *The Herald* office: 'Roast Bishop,' and the managing editor forwarded the order to me. I knew if I did not obey it I would be fired." I asked him if the order had been "Shoot Bishop" would he have obeyed it? For the honor of all the other press correspondents, let me add that all those who had been present at the conversation came to me in great indignation and denounced the man for his conduct, saying that they would ostracise him from their acquaintance, which they did. He died a short time later. He was a veritable black sheep in the fold, for the Washington correspondents, so far as my experience of them goes, are an exceptionally honorable body of men.

But what a picture of the Bennett kind of journalism the incident presents! Bennett had never known me, had nothing whatever against me, and yet, out of some crazy desire to injure Roosevelt whom he disliked, he ordered his paper to open fire on me, or rather start a fire under me. Roosevelt's contempt for the paper was fully justified by the incident, and his treatment of me in connection with it was only an item in a general course of action which he invariably followed toward all subordinates and associates whom he trusted. He always "stood by" them, and by so doing he bound them to him with a devotion which nothing could shake. By being inflexibly loyal to them, he made them equally loyal to himself.

And what a pleasure it was to transact official business with him! Not a second or a word was wasted. His abnormally rapid mental processes, and his ability to concentrate his mind absolutely on the subject under consideration, led to decision and action without delay. He saw the end of an argument long before it was reached, with a veritable feminine intuition, and would break in with: "I see, I see! You want so and so for the work—it is necessary to it—all right, give me the papers—I'll sign them now." I am naturally a concise talker and in every instance in which I went to him for action I made every effort possible to state my case briefly, but I never was able to finish. He got to the end before I could—and he always got

THEODORE ROOSEVELT

there, as one of his associates said of him, "with both feet." Charles J. Bonaparte, who served as Secretary of the Navy and Attorney-General in his Cabinet, estimated the rapidity of his mental processes at about ten times that of the ordinary man. I think this is a conservative estimate.

Soon after I became Secretary of the Canal Commission the question arose of providing means of recreation for the American employees on the Isthmus. There were no reputable places of amusement there, and the lack of these caused such discontent among the employees that it was difficult to maintain a permanent force. The annual changes amounted to 90 per cent. The Commission devised a plan providing recreation buildings or club-houses, to be erected, furnished and operated at the Government expense, in six of the largest settlements of workers. The cost was estimated at $35,000 each, with the expense of operation added. The legal counsel of the Commission, a strictly technical interpreter of the law, expressed the opinion that such use of the canal appropriations was of doubtful legality and that when the bills for proposed structures came before the Comptroller of the Treasury they might be disapproved. The Commission was at a standstill. I took the matter to President Roosevelt and explained to him the imperative need, physical and moral, of the buildings to the welfare of the employees and the progress of the work. He took the view that they were as necessary as were suitable living-quarters, good food, sanitation, and other objects of expenditure for the health and welfare of the force, since with a discontented and constantly changing force the best results could not be secured.

He asked me why the Commission did not go ahead at once and erect the buildings. When I informed him of the legal adviser's opinion, he exclaimed: "You go back and tell that man to keep his mouth shut. He is not there to find objections; let the other fellow do that. I want to build the canal; I do not want to be told how not to do it, but how to do it. You tell the Commission to go ahead and build the club-houses. I'll take the responsibility. If the Comptroller of the Treasury throws out the bills, I'll send a special message to Congress, asking for a special appropriation for the purpose. I will see to it that our boys down there are properly taken care of."

The club-houses were built, the Comptroller passed the bills without question, and no objection to the use of the money was ever raised in any quarter. Before the canal was completed there were five of these larger buildings, costing about $35,000 each and about $7,000 a year each for their operation, together with several smaller ones. They were the centres of social and athletic activities and contributed immeasurably to the well-being and contentment of the force, and, consequently, to the progress of the work.

After the club-houses were put in operation, their managers reported a growing demand for books among the members, and suggested the purchase of small libraries for each building, there being no libraries or collections of books for public use anywhere on the Isthmus. When this suggestion was taken up for consideration the legal adviser again raised the question of legality in connection with such use of the Government money. Again I went to President Roosevelt, stating the case to him, and saying that through inquiries to publishers and booksellers I had ascertained that I could purchase libraries of selected books, containing each 600 volumes, for $500 each. "Why don't you buy them?" he asked. I stated the legal adviser's opinion, whereupon he reiterated, with additional vigor, what he had said on the previous occasion about the functions of the legal adviser, and added: "You spend the money, buy the books, and tell the Commission I authorize the expenditure."

Again no objection was made by any one to this expenditure. The need was a real one. Later, when I was stationed on the Isthmus, I was informed by many members of the force that they had read every one of the books in the libraries, and the demand for more was so insistent that a small sum was set apart each year by the Commission for the purchase of additional volumes. The beneficial effects of the presence of the books for use in idle hours can scarcely be overestimated.

In both instances—securing the club-houses and the books—President Roosevelt's action was of incalculable value. If Congress had been asked for action, indefinite delay and inadequate provision, if not actual refusal, would have been the ultimate result.

One other, and even more important instance of the value of Roosevelt's prompt action in the case of the canal, action in which I was personally concerned, remains to be mentioned. On the eve of my sailing for permanent residence at Panama in July, 1907, Roosevelt summoned me to Oyster Bay for final instructions. He asked me, as soon as I became familiar with the situation there, to write him confidentially about it, stating what obstacles, if any, were hampering Colonel Goethals, and suggesting remedies, bidding me to assure the Colonel that he should back him up in everything. After I had been at Panama about a month, I wrote him a series of letters, defining the situation, saying the chief obstacle to progress, and a very serious one, was the cumbersome seven-headed Commission, and that the first essential to satisfactory progress was the placing of autocratic power and sole responsibility in the hands of Colonel Goethals. Immediately on receipt of this recommendation, the President replied that he agreed with me, and bade me tell the Colonel to have the necessary Executive Order drawn up and brought to him for signature. This the Colonel did and took it in person to Washington. He showed it to William H. Taft, who was then Secretary of War, and the member of the Cabinet in charge of canal work. The Secretary read it, said that he did not think it was entirely in accordance with law, but advised the Colonel to take it to the President. Colonel Goethals himself described, in an article which he published in *Scribner's Magazine*, in May, 1913, what took place when he reached the President:

"After reading it, the President reached for a pen, asking if it was satisfactory to me. I replied affirmatively, but explained that Mr. Taft thought that it was not exactly in accord with the law. To this the President replied that he would take his chances with the law, adding that he wanted the canal built."

The President then signed the Order, and of its effect, Colonel Goethals gave this estimate in the article from which I have quoted:

"Now that the Canal is in operation, I doubt if this result could have been accomplished in any other way than by a single responsible head. This President Roosevelt realized the first time I met him, and I have consequently felt that to this Order and to the support given to me in carrying it out are due the results that have been attained."

Roosevelt's action was criticized severely at the time, but his action, in this and in all other matters relating to the canal, was approved by Congress in the act which it passed for the operation of the canal after its completion.

CHAPTER IX

THEODORE ROOSEVELT
(CONTINUED)

DURING the two years of my residence in Washington I had many opportunities to see Roosevelt at close range, officially and otherwise, and I was never with him that he did not do or say something that was worth remembering. It was his custom each day at noon to pass from his private office into the adjoining Cabinet Room to greet visitors who had been assembled there during the morning to await his coming. There were usually a considerable number of these, fifty or more, and they were arranged, standing, on three sides of the room, the unoccupied side being that in which was the door leading to the President's office. As I usually had business to transact with him after the reception was over, I took my stand near the office door, or at the last end of the line. He would come in promptly, full of life and energy, first greeting the person nearest to him. On one occasion this person was a United States Senator who was waiting there to introduce two constituents. He introduced one, giving a German name, which sounded like Lubke, but that was not it. Roosevelt caught it and grasping the man by the hand, he said: "Mr. Lubke, I am delighted to see you. Your family comes from (naming the place) in Germany, doesn't it?" The man, quite astonished, said it did. Whereupon Roosevelt proceeded to tell him as much if not more about his family than he had ever known, and he admitted it was all true and his joy and pride were visible in his face. Then the Senator introduced the other constituent, giving his name. This man was wearing a Legion of Honor button. Roosevelt touched it, saying: "Mr. Blank, your regiment was (naming its State and number) and you were in the battles of so and so," giving a list of a half-dozen or more. In each instance he was right, and the second visitor's emotions were equal to those of the first. All this had taken only a few minutes, but the whole room was excited and amazed by it. Then the President started around the room, passing swiftly from one person to another, saying something to each that left pleasure behind it, and so on till the end of the line. It was all over in an incredibly short time, but every one was pleased. When women and children were present, his success with them was greatest of all. They had literally to be pushed out of the room by the attendants, for they hung back at the doorway, desiring to get the utmost possible view of him.

I took to the room one day an important financial man from New York who had wished to meet the President personally. We stationed ourselves in my usual place at the end of the line, and were witnesses to all that passed. Just before the President reached us a man to whom he had extended his hand stepped out of the line and began to say something to him in a low tone. Roosevelt stepped back, held up his hand and said: "No, no, my friend, you must not do that! You don't mean to do anything improper, but you are doing that. I know what your case is. You sent me your papers, and I have turned them over to the Attorney-General for an opinion and recommendation. When he returns them to me I shall act upon his findings. You see I am in the position of a judge in the matter. If you had a case in court you would not think of speaking to the judge about it when he was off the bench, would you? I am sure you would not. I am very glad to see you, good day." All this was perfectly audible to every one in the room, and done with such amiability that even the visitor himself could not complain of his treatment. When we emerged to the street my New York friend was full of admiration for what he had witnessed. "What a man!" he exclaimed. "I have never seen anything like him. It is all nonsense for him to say he will not accept another term. The country cannot afford to lose him." It was a cold day in midwinter, and my enraptured friend stood with bared head as he said this. "In the meantime," said I, "hadn't you better put on your hat?" He had forgotten that he had not done so.

Still another occasion. The first man to be greeted was a United States Senator who asked the President if he could see him privately for a moment. Roosevelt, very cheerful, replied: "Oh, that's not necessary, we can talk freely here. You want to see me about that man you wish me to appoint. I can't do it, Senator; and I will tell you why." And he proceeded to do so with a frankness that made the Senator speechless with wrath, for the revelation was most unpleasant to him.

His comments in private conversation on persons for whom, for one reason or another, he had little use, were forcible and original. Of one man, whose record I had looked up at his request, he said, when I made my report: "Yes, yes, I see. If he were a horse we would call him a 'skate.'" Of another he said: "I have tried in vain to do business with him, but it is impossible. He has an intellect of eight-guinea-pig power—of the mutton-suet variety." Coming from a social gathering where he had been bored beyond endurance, and was looking unusually fierce, he said, when asked if anything was troubling him: "I have been trying to be tactful!"

When I called at his office one day he was engaged with an official who finished his business with him as I arrived. "Is that all?" asked the President. "Yes, I think it is," was the reply, and as an after-thought the visitor added: "Oh, by the way, so and so of the Navy is a candidate for promotion by you, I believe. He is a fine fellow and I hope you will see your way clear to promote him." With set teeth and a heavy frown, the President turned on him: "Now, who put you up to saying that? You are the third or fourth man who has come to me with that talk during the past few days. If I thought the man himself was sending them, by George! I would not promote him. I don't like the looks of it."

One evening I was summoned to the White House for a consultation on a phase of canal affairs. Among others present were two venerable and notoriously adroit members of the Senate. As we were leaving at the close of the meeting I started to follow the Senators. As I took the President's hand he held me back for a moment till they had passed from the room, and whispered: "Let those two old foxes go first." On another occasion when he had several Senators present I asked him, after we were alone, why he had omitted Senator Platt. "Because," he replied, "we had a serious question to consider and Platt would have turned the meeting into a row about a post-office."

His ability to concentrate his mind upon one subject to the exclusion of all others was literally phenomenal. When he was reading a document or a book or a newspaper, nothing could distract his attention. It was useless to speak to him for he neither heard nor saw you. When the Senate, under the lead of Senator Foraker of Ohio, made an attack upon him for his punishment of the negro troops engaged in the Brownsville, Texas, riots, I expressed some sympathy for him because of the annoyance it might be causing him. "Oh," he said, "that is merely the latest log going down the stream!" Several months later he published in *The Century* magazine an article on "The Ancient Irish Sagas," which showed great research and profound knowledge of the subject. I asked him how he had been able to find time for such a study. "I have always been interested in the subject," he replied, "and when the Brownsville row started in the Senate I knew it would be a long and possibly irritating business if I followed it; so I shut myself up, paid no heed to the row, and wrote the article."

The scope of his reading included the whole field of human knowledge. It was nearly or quite impossible to mention any work of serious literary or historical importance which he had not read. Time and again I said to him that I had just read a book that I thought he would like. When I named it, the invariable reply was: "Oh, I have read that"; and then he would proceed to give me a digest of its contents which was so comprehensive as to convince me that I had not read it carefully. He had not only read that particular book, but several others on the same subject. "Were you ever able to mention a book to the President that he had not read?" a lady asked me at a dinner in the White House. When I answered in the negative, she continued: "I have dined here many times and talked much with him, and I have never discovered a book that was unknown to him. On one occasion I thought I had found one which he surely could not have seen. It was a rare book by an Icelandic author, and I came here confident that I should at last be able to tell the President something that he did not know. Luckily, I found myself seated next to him at table and when what seemed to be the opportune moment came, I said: 'Mr. President, are you interested in Icelandic literature?' With a bounce in his chair he turned an eager countenance upon me and said: 'Am I not!' and then proceeded to tell me not only all about my one lonely Icelandic book but dozens of others that I had never heard of."

I sat one evening with him and some friends in his library when the talk ran on historical writing and a casual remark was made about original views in such writing. Roosevelt, who had been sitting quietly, sprang from his chair, exclaiming, "What do you mean by original views in history?" He then began walking up and down the room, and, starting with the dawn of written history, he came swinging down from epoch to epoch, citing authors and rulers and dates in each, with the peculiarities of writers and subjects and with a fluency and accuracy simply astounding. For an hour this marvellous display went on, while we sat spellbound. Whatever he read was stamped in-

THEODORE ROOSEVELT

delibly upon his memory and was ready at all times to his command. He loved historical writing best of all, but his enjoyment of that did not prevent him from taking keen delight in other branches of literature. Especially did he delight in "Alice in Wonderland" and "Through the Looking Glass" and "The Hunting of the Snark," and in nonsense verses of various kinds. He was fond of quoting these, often to the astonishment and mystification of those who heard him. When a far-Western Senator called on him in regard to an appointment to office, he was both mystified and disgusted by the query: "Senator, did you ever read 'The Hunting of the Snark'?" The Senator, who was familiar with wild animals in his region but who had never heard of a snark, admitted that he had not read the story. "Well, Senator, in that story the Bellman says: 'I have said it three times. What I tell you three times is true.' I have told you three times that I cannot appoint your man, and it is true."

As I have said, Roosevelt always denied that he had genius and usually he coupled the denial with an assertion that he was not an orator. This was true in the early years of his public life. Later he was one of the most effective political orators of his time. He had found himself and filled

NOTES AND ANECDOTES

completely the definition which Lord Morley put in his "Life of Gladstone": "Political oratory is action, not words—action, character, will, conviction, purpose, personality." All these qualities were seen and recognized by every political audience that Roosevelt appeared before from the time he became President till the end of his life. It was Roosevelt the man that the audience saw and heard. He was in action before it. The Archbishop of York, Primate of England, when he was visiting the United States in 1918, said that the greatest oratorical success he had ever witnessed was scored by Roosevelt in 1910 when he was speaking in England before an audience of 700 graduates in the Cambridge Union. His introducer on that occasion had spoken of Roosevelt as a man who had borne the burdens of office as the head of a great nation. Roosevelt began his speech with a denial that his burdens had been heavy, and striding forward, with clenched fist raised high in the air, exclaimed: "I liked my job!" That entirely foreign audience saw the man behind that declaration and hailed him with uproarious delight.

I have sat behind him on the platform many times when he was speaking and the audience always presented the same marvellous spectacle.

THEODORE ROOSEVELT

Literally every eye was fastened on him and every countenance displayed intense and unbroken interest in what he was saying. I sat thus in Carnegie Hall, on the evening of Oct. 28, 1918, when he made the last speech of his life. He spoke for two hours and a quarter and not a soul left the hall till the end and there was not a moment during which he lost his complete and fairly entranced hold upon the audience. I could not detect a single person in the vast throng whose gaze wavered from him during the entire speech. He was in action every minute, though he had come to the hall with an inflamed foot which had been heavily bandaged to enable him to stand upon it. His first deliverance won every soul in the audience, for as he arose to speak a voice high up in the gallery shouted: "Three cheers for the fighting man!" Quick as a flash, Roosevelt's hand went up, and amid dense silence he said sternly: "Don't cheer for me. I'd have been in the fight if I had been allowed. Cheer for the fighting man at the front and let us see that his blood is not shed in vain!" The response to that almost burst the walls of the building. The whole of Lord Morley's definition of political oratory was in that one sentence. Later, when in giving a list of the men of various nationalities who had taken part in our Civil War he mentioned that "brilliant Irish soldier, Phil Sheridan," and the audience broke into applause, he looked up from his manuscript with a broad smile and said: "That's good. Cheer away. I am part Irish myself." A pandemonium of cheers and laughter followed. That was again Roosevelt in action—his personality in full sight. I have heard many eloquent orators but none who had such perfect control of an audience as Roosevelt.

During my seven years' service at Panama I saw Roosevelt only during my annual vacations in the United States and then mainly for official business. Soon after the expiration of my service I said to him that I was looking for some occupation, when he replied: "I know what I wish you would do—write the story of my public life. You know it almost as well as I know it myself. I will turn all my official and private correspondence over to you for your exclusive control." We talked much about the project then and subsequently and a few years before he died we had evolved a plan and I began the task. We agreed that as far as possible the story should be told in his own letters and this was done. From the beginning of the work I consulted him at frequent intervals and when he died the greater part of a draft of the first volume had been read and approved by him. Occasionally he would say when a passage in a letter severely criticised some public man: "Cut that out. His descendants are living and I don't wish to hurt their feelings. Besides it has no bearing on the narrative." This was the only excision he ever requested.

During his later years, when he was frequently in the hospital, he read my manuscript while lying in bed, and though I knew he was often suffering severe pain, he never spoke of it, for then, as always, he bore in silence whatever affliction he might have. Well and intimately as I knew him, I did not know that he had lost the sight of one eye till many years after it had gone.

In my visits at the hospital we talked occasionally of politics. When President Wilson appointed his commissioners for the Paris Peace Conference, in November, 1918, he said to me on the day the names were published: "Wilson has made a great mistake. His friends say he is a shrewd politician. He is not, and these selections prove it. If he were a shrewd politician he would not, in the first place, go himself to Paris. As President in Washington he is the most powerful ruler in the world to-day, but when he leaves Washington and goes to Paris he strips himself of his great power.

NOTES AND ANECDOTES

In the second place, he should have appointed Root as one of the commissioners. If he had done that he would have secured for himself Root's great ability. I know Root. He is first and always a lawyer. From the moment he had been appointed Root would have regarded himself as Wilson's retained counsel and his service would have been of incalculable value to Wilson in many ways. It would have given him a wise councillor and, most valuable of all, Root's standing as a Republican and a former Senator would have prevented Republican criticism and opposition in the Senate which is sure to come." The wisdom of that comment was fully confirmed by subsequent events.

During the closing months of 1918 the sentiment in the Republican party in Roosevelt's favor became so strong as to assure his nomination, virtually unanimously, as its candidate for the Presidency in 1920. When I told him of this, only a short time before his death, he said, rather sadly:

"I am indifferent to the subject. I would not lift a finger to get the nomination. Since Quentin's death the world seems to have shut down upon me. My other boys are on the other side of the water fighting, or being made ready to fight for their country. If they do not come back, what

THEODORE ROOSEVELT

would the Presidency mean to me? At best I have only a few remaining years, and nothing could give me greater joy than to spend them with my family. I have been President for seven years and I am not eager to be President again. But if the leaders of the party come to me and say that they are convinced that I am the man the people want and the only man who can be elected, and that they are all for me, I don't see how I could refuse to run. If I do consent, it will be because as President I could accomplish some things that I should like to see accomplished before I die." This he had said quietly while lying back on his pillows. Then, sitting suddenly erect and clenching his fist, the old fighting Roosevelt reappeared in the declaration: "And by George, if they take me, they will take me without a single reservation or modification of the things I have always stood for!"

The last time I saw him was on the afternoon of the day before Christmas, 1918. He was sitting in a chair and was to leave the hospital on the next morning for Oyster Bay. He went over the typewritten manuscript for the book of his "Letters to His Children" which I had prepared for publication. As he finished reading the letters, he said: "I would rather have that book

NOTES AND ANECDOTES

published than anything that has ever been written about me." Surely, nothing that has been written about him, or may hereafter be written, can portray him to the world as he stands portrayed there. He had revealed himself freely with no thought that what he was writing would ever pass beyond the vision of his own family.

When I was going through his correspondence for my story of his public life I had come upon copies of his letters written from the White House to his boys when they were in school. In one of our talks I said to him that I had found these and that I considered them quite worth reproducing but that I did not see how I could put them in the book we were making. "Oh," replied he, "put two or three of them in an appendix." He was one of the few persons I have ever known who read appendices; he actually loved them and put them into many of his books. I objected in this instance, saying: "And bury them from all human eyes! Nobody except you ever looks at an appendix. I refuse to bury these letters there."

As I pursued my reading of the correspondence, I found more of the letters and had copies made of a dozen or more. These I took to him, asking him to read them, saying: "When you have read them I will tell you something I have in mind."

THEODORE ROOSEVELT

After he had read a few, he exclaimed, with characteristic frankness: "By George! these *are* pretty good. I had forgotten all about them." After he had finished he asked me what it was I had to say. I told him I wished to make a separate book of them. He was silent for a time and then said: "I don't know but that I would like to have you do it." As other letters came to hand he grew more interested and soon became heartily in favor of publication, saying that there were at Oyster Bay some earlier letters that he had written to the children when they were small, known in the family as "picture letters," because of crude illustrations which he had drawn in them. These were secured and were included in the book which was published after his death and has become a classic. It commanded a very large sale, which continues, and called forth a great volume of private letters of approval, including many from writers who said that it had completely changed their estimate of the man, that they had been his political enemies in the past but that they had never understood him till now and were free to confess that they had misjudged him.

His deep and abiding love of his children and the keen enjoyment which he took in sharing their games and sports these letters reveal. He loved not only his own but all children, for he was a boy in spirit till the end of his days. Several years after he had retired from the Presidency and was engaged in magazine writing an incident occurred which illustrated this side of his nature. He was at the time rapidly regaining his former position as a leader of public opinion and his magazine office was thronged daily by visitors who came from all parts of the country for personal interviews with him. On one occasion when the anteroom was crowded with persons, many of them political leaders, awaiting their turns to see him, a great tumult inside the office became audible. There were hoarse growls and shrieks of childish laughter which excited astonishment and curiosity. What could be going on in that room? Inside information disclosed later the fact that Finley Peter Dunne (Mr. Dooley) had brought his small son to see Colonel Roosevelt, and the ex-President was on all fours on the floor "playing bear" with him, in complete disregard of the callers who were more or less patiently awaiting audience.

I read all his correspondence, estimated by his secretaries at 150,000 letters, and in all that mass I found not a single letter that needed to be suppressed in order to spare his fame from blemish.

THEODORE ROOSEVELT

There is not a single letter among all these that he wrote to the politicians of his party, its leaders and bosses, or to anyone else, in which he reveals the slightest deviation from his professed high standards of political conduct. He worked with politicians, but when the time for action came they bowed to his demands; he never yielded to them on a question of principle. Confirmation of this statement of mine, if confirmation be asked, was found in the Barnes libel suit, when such fierce and meticulous search as was never made in any other public man's correspondence was made in his and failed to discover a single compromising or discrediting line or sentence. As he himself said: "Do you know what meant more to me than anything else in the trial? There was no single thing in all those old letters of mine that I am ashamed to have my children read." He could have said the same of all his other letters. I know, because I have read them.

He was the same man in his letters that he was in daily life, unaffected, direct and frank. He never wrote a stilted or artificial or vainglorious letter and never displayed those qualities in social or official intercourse. There was not a trace of personal vanity in him. He talked and wrote freely about what he was doing and expressed frankly his joy in the success of his efforts, but his rejoicing was always because of the results which he had been able to secure and never took the form of self-glorification. Underneath it all was a devout thankfulness that he had been able to exert the power given him for the accomplishment of worthy purposes. He was an idealist but not a futilist—if I may coin the word. "Mind you," he said to me many times, "I will get the ideal result if I can, but if I can't get the ideal I'll get the nearest to it possible. I will not refuse to get any result at all simply because I can't get the ideal one." He had no patience with those persons who spend their energies in support of hopeless causes. "If your conscience compels you to throw away your vote in every election," he was fond of saying, "I advise you to examine it and see if it is healthy."

He hitched his wagon to a star, but he was careful to have the rope long enough to keep its wheels on the earth. He was a born crusader but not a Don Quixote. He was the eager, unresting, unswerving champion of the things that ought to be, with a devotion that was a religion, a sincerity that neither yielded nor faltered, a love for the welfare of his fellow men, and a human sympathy with them which was boundless and inexhaustible.

THEODORE ROOSEVELT

Lowell said of Lincoln: "I consider it a benediction to have lived in the same country and in the same time with Abraham Lincoln." So, with a full and grateful heart, I say that I consider it a benediction to have lived in the same country and in the same time with Theodore Roosevelt and to have had the priceless gift of his friendship.

CHAPTER X

FRIENDS OF MANY KINDS

SOME of the most pleasurable of my memories are of men of diverse professions and occupations with whom I had comparatively brief but none the less enjoyable association. One of them was Sir Henry Irving. I saw much of him during his several professional visits to this country, and found him a delightful companion. His chief charm in private life as well as on the stage was his intellectuality. He disliked to talk about his profession, saying to each new acquaintance that he would talk with him about anything except the theatre. And he talked like the intellectual man he was most interestingly on many subjects, especially English politics, English literature, English public men and history. One saw clearly where he got the intellectual quality which dominated his acting. He had studied thoroughly the literature of each character and all that related to it. If an author was mentioned with whom he was not familiar, and who was said to have written about one of his characters, he at once made a note of author and work.

FRIENDS OF MANY KINDS

While he showed obvious dislike of personal praise of his acting, he welcomed any appreciation of a play itself in which he had a part. On one occasion when I was at supper with him after a performance of Tennyson's *Becket*, I spoke of the vision scene in the monastery, saying I thought it struck a higher note than anything I had ever seen on the stage. What I meant, but did not say, was that he had struck that note. He at once assumed that I was not speaking of his acting by saying: "The soliloquy is beautiful, isn't it? *Becket's* vision of his childhood, when the love and sweetness of his youth come back to him?" That the part appealed to him was evident in the way he spoke of it, and he showed that my appreciation of it had pleased him by sending me a few days later a photograph of himself as *Becket* inscribed: "With cordial greeting—Henry Irving."

On another occasion, when some one was speaking of Wolsey's "Farewell! a long farewell to all my greatness," Irving, with a sardonic smile, said: "And I am told that schoolboys in the United States deliver that soliloquy better than I do! And they do *declaim* it better. Wolsey had just been condemned, thrown from power and despoiled by the king. He was speaking as an utterly crushed and beaten man. Under such conditions a man's speech is full of agony, is broken, at times almost inarticulate—he does not *declaim.*" I quote from memory, and while the words are not entirely his the substance is accurate.

He was the most charming of hosts, for he had a genius for friendship and delighted in hospitality. At small dinners, given to a few chosen friends on Sunday evenings in the old familiar Red Room at Delmonico's, on Madison Square, now, alas, no more! he was at his best. There he would drop sometimes into reminiscence, not about himself, but about other personages in the theatrical profession, and his anecdotes, told with great simplicity, were always the gems of the evening.

He had one about an old theatrical manager who, he told us, was a famous character in London in his day. He had earned a competence, had retired, and had bought a little place in the suburbs of London which he had fixed up to suit himself and his wife and in which they were to pass a calm and happy old age. Barely had he got the place to suit them when he fell ill, took to his bed and, becoming alarmed, sent for a physician whom he asked anxiously what was the matter with him. The physician answered that he was a very sick man. "How sick?" he asked. "Do you

FRIENDS OF MANY KINDS

wish me to tell you?" "Yes." "Well, you have only a very short time to live and I advise you if you wish to see a clergyman to send for one without delay." "Do you mean that?" "I certainly do; there is no chance whatever for your recovery." The old fellow looked searchingly at the doctor for a moment, then flopped over with his face to the wall, and said: "Well, all I've got to say is it's a d——d shame!"

An amusing incident occurred at a dinner which Irving gave at Delmonico's during one of his visits to the United States. There were 75 or 100 persons present, for he had a host of American friends who had fairly overwhelmed him with hospitality. As I went into the banquet hall with him he said in confidence: "I am not going to have any speeches. Every speaker thinks he must praise me—and I am tired of being called to my face the 'greatest living ac-tor'!"

Shortly before the end of the *menu* was reached, he rose and said that he was going to venture upon the violation of what he knew was a sacred American tradition—he was going to ask that there be no speeches. He had invited them to be present with him because he wished to show appreciation of the many courteous and friendly acts they had showered upon him, and he thought that the evening could be made most enjoyable if they were to move about and talk informally with one another.

As soon as he resumed his seat, a guest of incurable after-dinner oratorical propensities, who was obviously big with speech, arose and said that he was quite sure that all his fellow guests would take pleasure in acquiescing in their distinguished host's wishes, but he was quite sure also that his host would waive his objection to speeches sufficiently to permit of a few words from the Nestor of journalism who was present and in whose English, pure and undefiled, all found such unending delight.

It happened that at one end of the long table on the dais, in the centre of which Irving sat, Charles A. Dana was placed and at the other end, Parke Godwin. Both arose simultaneously at the call for a Nestor, each unconscious that the other was up. Mr. Dana, being a little more nimble, began to speak first. When the sound of his voice reached Mr. Godwin who was visibly collecting his thoughts, the expression of astonishment, not to say dismay, that passed over his countenance at this revelation of the presence of another Nestor in the field, was irresistibly comic. The scene was in full view of the body of guests

FRIENDS OF MANY KINDS

seated in front of the platform, but neither Irving nor Mr. Dana was aware of it. The latter was obviously much astonished at the tremendous outburst of laughter which greeted a remark of very mild jocosity which he made early in his speech, not knowing that the cause of the explosion was the bewildered countenance of the rival Nestor who had resumed his seat at the other end of the table.

Irving had a faculty of saying a great deal in a few words, or even a single word. He attended what was called an "All-Star" performance of the *Rivals* which was given in New York during one of his visits. Meeting him after it I asked him his opinion of the performance of William H. Crane, a broad-comedy actor who had taken the part of *Sir Anthony Absolute*. After a moment's hesitation he replied: "Agricultural." In like manner he had said, when asked what he thought of Wilson Barrett's *Hamlet*: "Voluble, voluble!" Barrett was an actor of the explosive-utterance type whose speech sounded like the explosion of a bunch of firecrackers.

For several years I was a member of a dining club that met monthly during the winter season. Among my fellow members were Charles Francis

NOTES AND ANECDOTES

Adams, the second of the name, Woodrow Wilson, Joseph H. Choate, and Wayne MacVeagh. Mr. Adams was a source of constant pleasure to me, both at the club dinners and elsewhere, for we were friends for many years. He was the most disputatious, not to say cantankerous, person I have ever known. He fairly revelled in contradiction, and was never more happy than when he had an entire company in opposition to him in a controversy. One has only to read his "Autobiography," among the most entertaining of its class, to realize this.

I once consulted him on an incident in the history of the Adams family which I wished to include in a book I was writing. I said to him that I was interested in the fact that the only two Presidents in our history who had refused to attend the inauguration of their successors were Adamses—John, who had left Washington early in the morning to avoid the inauguration of Jefferson, and John Quincy, in the same manner, to avoid that of Jackson. "And quite properly, too!" exclaimed Charles Francis. Then I went on to say that the Adams family had made valuable contributions to American history through diaries and letters: John Adams in his partial diary supplemented by his letters to his wife, and

FRIENDS OF MANY KINDS

John Quincy Adams through his immortal diary which was a mine of information. "Never ought to have been published," exclaimed Charles Francis. "The man was not in good health, had indigestion, and wrote down a lot of rubbish. This diary business is all nonsense anyway. Look at old Pepys! See what a figure he cuts!" Nothing daunted, I continued: "You are editing your father's diary, which will continue the history down till later times. How do you find that?" "Stupidest thing you ever saw," was the reply.

When I related these observations to John Hay, when he was Secretary of State, he laughed and said: "There is nothing like the Adams family. A few weeks ago I was giving a dinner to an illustrious Englishman who was visiting this country, and as Charles Francis Adams was in town, I invited him. When I presented him to the Englishman the latter said: 'Oh, Mr. Adams, I am glad to meet you. I had the very great pleasure of coming over on the same steamer with your brother Henry.' 'I should not like to have done that,' exclaimed Charles Francis. A few days ago," continued Hay, "Henry Adams came into my office and, throwing himself into a chair, remarked: 'I have just seen my brother Brooks off to Europe. He can't make a d——d fool of himself again in this country for six weeks at least.' "

One night at dinner I was seated next to Woodrow Wilson, who was then President of Princeton University. It was at the time of the Russian-Japanese war, and he was deeply interested in the conflict. He said to me very earnestly: "You are a close friend of President Roosevelt. Why don't you go down to Washington and impress it upon him that it is his duty to take the side of Russia in this war?" "Do you mean interfere in the name of our Government?" "Yes," he replied. "On what ground?" I asked. "On the ground of civilization and the welfare of mankind." "Wilson," I said, "you amaze and confound me. 'On the ground of civilization' with Russia—the most anti-civilized autocracy in Europe. Why, only a month ago you told me you were anti-imperialist in regard to the Philippines—that we ought to come away from them and leave them to their fate—that we had no business to be a world-power, and that we have troubles enough at home. Now you want us to go around the world and interfere in a war which is none of our business." Without paying the slightest heed to what I said, Wilson went on repeating and emphasizing his statements.

FRIENDS OF MANY KINDS

In the midst of his talk I heard the voice of Wayne MacVeagh from the far side of the table, saying to Charles Francis Adams: "I tell you, Adams, there is only one course for this Government to take and that is to take the side of Japan in this war in the name of civilization." I called to him to come over to my side and argue the matter out with Wilson, saying what his position was. "Oh," said MacVeagh, as he came to us, "I'm only baiting Adams." Wilson was not baiting me, but was in earnest. What impressed me most about him was his absolute refusal to pay any heed to my words, either in regard to his complete about-face of attitude, or in any other way. In after years, when he was President of the United States, I realized that this was a fixed habit with him.

MacVeagh's "baiting of Adams" did not disturb that gentleman in the least. He rather enjoyed the proceeding. I have seen him under fire from an entire company, spending the whole evening in an unbroken wrangle, and have received a few days later a letter from him saying: "What an enjoyable evening we had!" He had contradicted everybody and everybody had contradicted him. Once when he astonished me by saying: "You are talking sense. That's what

NOTES AND ANECDOTES

I think," I exclaimed: "Adams, I have known you for a quarter of a century, and you have never agreed with me before. You shake my confidence in the soundness of my own views." He smiled as if I had paid him a compliment and we were better friends than ever. It was impossible for any one who knew him well not to be his friend and not to have for him both esteem and affection, for he was a man.

Joseph H. Choate I knew in a friendly but not intimate way for many years. I was familiar with him as an after-dinner speaker in whom the whole city took delight, as a wit who had few equals, and as a brilliant lawyer who stood in the front rank of his profession. Thackeray said of a gracious and beautiful woman that to see her walk to her carriage was a holiday. To hear Choate speak at a great banquet was always a holiday. Every requisite for supreme success was his—the tall, commanding figure, with its large, finely moulded head and refined, intellectual face; the rich, musical, well-modulated voice; the easy flow of perfectly chosen words; the constant play of delicious humor, and unvaryingly an exquisite lightness of touch that was peculiarly his own. Added to these attributes was a gift for impudence

FRIENDS OF MANY KINDS

in personal allusions which was as diverting as it frequently was audacious, but which left no sting even among its victims.

One of his greatest successes that I witnessed was at a banquet where, as often was the case, he and Chauncey M. Depew were pitted together as speakers. Mr. Depew, who was a popular after-dinner orator of quite a different type, had spoken first and had poked some mild fun at Choate. When the latter rose to follow him he began by saying very quietly that previous to coming to the banquet he had received a very interesting circular which he would read. It was the prospectus of a natural gas company. He read it soberly through and then added: "This circular is signed: 'Depew Natural Gas Company, Limited.'" Raising his eyes from the paper, and looking over the audience with an air of innocent bewilderment, he asked: "Why limited?" The effect was tremendous and irrepressible, for at intervals the audience broke into uncontrollable laughter during the rest of the evening.

He was fond of jibing at Depew at every opportunity. On one occasion he was requested, at short notice, to replace Depew at a banquet at which the latter had been announced as a speaker and had been prevented at the last moment from attending. When he was introduced as Depew's substitute, Choate began his remarks by saying: "I appear before you, gentlemen, with my sides torn and bleeding from the spur of opportunity."

Countless anecdotes of him are told by his contemporaries and during his lifetime there was scarcely a day in which one or more of Choate's witticisms did not pass eagerly from mouth to mouth. I will mention a few only which I know to be authentic. He was at one time inspecting a new court-room for the Bankruptcy Court which was nearing completion. The person who was showing him about said that everything was finished with the exception of a suitable motto to put above the judge's chair, and asked Choate if he could suggest one. He at once replied that he could, saying they should go to the Scriptures, the fountainhead for all such things. Asked to specify one, he, mindful of the nationality of the great body of litigants in that court, replied: "He that keepeth Israel shall neither slumber nor sleep."

He was once arguing a case before a court over which a judge was presiding who was notorious for his somewhat discourteous conduct toward counsel. Noticing that the judge was obviously paying slight heed to his argument, Choate

FRIENDS OF MANY KINDS

paused and remained silent for a few moments. The judge asked him why he had stopped. With perfect serenity Choate said: "I know what is passing in your Honor's mind." "What do you mean, sir?" asked the judge. Choate, still suave and deferential, said: "The Constitution stipulates that the court shall hear causes. It nowhere stipulates that the court shall listen."

A constitutional convention of the State of New York was held several years ago in the Assembly Chamber of the State Capitol at Albany. A few years after the building had been erected, the stone ceiling of the Chamber, through defective construction, had fallen, and had been replaced. Choate was the president of the convention and was in the chair when a member with an abnormally loud voice was using it in full power in a speech. As he paused for a moment, Choate, suave as usual, said: "The chair begs to remind the gentleman that the ceiling of this chamber has fallen once."

I was only once in close association with him as a lawyer in a case in court. A newspaper with which I was connected was sued for libel for making, through misinformation, a false and unjustifiable charge against a firm of publishers. The charge was that the firm in question had published a pirated edition of Bryce's "American

Commonwealth," without consent of the author and without compensation to him. The fact was that the publication had been made in accordance with an agreement with the author. The newspaper had not a leg to stand on. It retained Choate as counsel. The publication occurred in the days before international copyright had been secured and the firm in question had been guilty of a long series of piracies of English books. At its head was a clergyman whom I will call the Reverend Doctor Blank.

In the trial Choate put this man on the stand and went over his acts of literary piracy mercilessly and in detail, showing the jury that if he had not been guilty of pirating this particular book he had pirated a host of others. When he came to his final argument, Choate's audacity fairly took one's breath away. He reviewed the evidence and said: "And who is it, gentlemen of the jury, who gives us this picture of the Reverend Doctor Blank and the Reverend Doctor Blank's business? Why, the Reverend Doctor Blank himself." Then advancing upon the Reverend Doctor, he fairly thrust his finger in his face and exclaimed: "Ecce Homo!" Pausing for a moment, he continued: "And, gentlemen of the jury, if there is one book which you would think a Doctor of Divinity would refrain from stealing it is a 'Life of Christ.' And yet, gentlemen of the jury, this Reverend Doctor Blank did not hesitate to make money out of the blood of his Redeemer!"

And he won the case for the newspaper, for the jury found in its favor.

My last experience with Choate occurred only a short time before his death. It was during the great World War. I went to him to ask him to make a speech at a mass-meeting of protest against the deportation and enslavement of Belgians by the Germans. He said he did not feel equal to making a speech but would gladly write a letter. I suggested, when he asked about the most desirable subject, that he write on the International Law of the case, saying that he had been at the Hague Conference and was familiar with that. We looked up the published records of the Conference and could find nothing applying specifically to the case. As we finished, he said: "Mr. Bishop, there is no law, international or other, to justify what Germany is doing, except the law of Satan."

I saw Bret Harte quite often in the old *Tribune* days when he came into the editorial rooms to chat with John Hay. He was very quiet in manner and speech and in my youthful eyes was quite fascinating. Many years later I met him at a luncheon which was given to Kipling during one of the latter's visits to the United States. After the luncheon the company sat about informally and some one raised the question of compliments to authors. Various anecdotes bearing on the point were related and among them one by Bret Harte which I, encouraged by Owen Wister's famous example in the "Virginian," will venture to reproduce here. Readers of that immortal story will remember that Mr. Wister said that until he visited cowboy land he had heard a certain expression used only as a "term of heaviest insult," and that he was astonished when he heard it applied to his hero as "language that was plainly complimentary," the secret as given by the "Virginian," being: "When you call me that, smile." In this version it appears in Harte's anecdote. I quote him from memory, but with substantial accuracy:

"Shortly after the publication of my first book, 'The Luck of Roaring Camp,' I had occasion to go to a little town in the Far West on a matter of business. When I got off the train at the small station there was only one man on the platform. He was in full cowboy costume, slouch hat, flannel shirt, highboots and spurs, pistol in belt, etc. He gave a start when I appeared, as if he had

FRIENDS OF MANY KINDS

been looking for me. When I went to the shack that did duty as the hotel in the town he followed me. I secured a room, went to it and, after washing and leaving my luggage, came down to the dining-room for supper. All the time I was eating, he kept walking back and forth looking at me through the door. I finished and went out into the office, or public-room, and lighted a cigar. My inquisitive stranger was still eyeing me closely and I was becoming somewhat nervous though I tried to appear calm and unconcerned. Suddenly he walked up to me and said: 'Are you Bret Harte!' I answered that I was. Somewhat eagerly came the next question: 'Did you write "The Outcasts of Poker Flat"?' When I replied yes, he threw wide his arms, clasping me in them, and exclaimed: 'You d——d old s—— of a b——!'

"That," said Bret Harte, "was the most satisfactory compliment I ever received."

Having been guilty of one anecdotal indiscretion, I may be pardoned if I venture on two others. Let me premise by saying that the English speak quite freely about matters which are considered not entirely suitable for polite conversation in this country. I was one evening at a musicale in Washington at which the guests were drawn from the most exclusive official circles.

NOTES AND ANECDOTES

The time was immediately following the celebrated Booker Washington dinner at the White House. After the musical programme had ended I was talking with a group of ladies when the British Ambassador sauntered up to us and, without the slightest idea that he was saying anything unusual, asked: "Oh, did you hear the delightful remark of the darky bishop who was preaching in Charleston on the Booker Washington incident? He said: 'There are 800,000 people in this country who don't know whether they are white or black—and *who done it?*'"

While I was living in Washington there came to take up residence in the city a newly wedded couple, the bride of which had just emerged from divorce proceedings that had been the foremost scandal of the land for several weeks. Washington society was agog with the question as to whether the newcomers should be permitted to "break in." I was sitting one evening with my family at dinner in a hotel restaurant which was filled with people among whom were many diplomats and other representatives of the official set. At the table next to mine sat an attaché of the British Embassy with his wife. She was one of the most charming women in Washington, brilliant, witty, and rarely gifted with conversational

FRIENDS OF MANY KINDS

powers. During a lull in the general talk, she turned suddenly to me and in a voice distinctly audible in all parts of the room, for she spoke with the clear and musical tones so admirable in the women of her race, said: "Oh, Mr. Bishop, I was out to dinner last evening when the conversation turned on the famous Mrs. Blank, and the question of the number of co-respondents in her divorce case was raised. The number reported ranged from six to a dozen. Whereupon the Swiss Minister made a delightful remark to me: 'After two, you know, it really doesn't matter!'"

As I write these reminiscences of Washington social life two anecdotes come to my mind which were related to me by a former member of President Cleveland's cabinet. He found himself at an official dinner seated next to the wife of an attaché of the German Embassy who was a recent arrival in Washington. In the course of the dinner terrapin was served. When a plate of it was placed before this lady, she carefully averted her eyes from it, reached for a piece of bread which she crumbled and placed over the terrapin, completely covering it from sight. Her neighbor, having only the slightest acquaintance with her, refrained from comment on this curious action. Some weeks later, after he had met her several times and had come to know her sufficiently to justify his query, he alluded to her conduct and asked her the reason for it. She replied: "Why, you know what they told me you made it of! They told me you made it of little niggers' toes!" Like many other new arrivals from foreign parts, ready and eager to believe any sort of wild yarn about Americans, the poor lady had been the victim of the rollicking young bucks about the foreign legations whose chief delight is found in supplying information of that sort.

The second anecdote supplied by the same Cabinet member related to the perplexities of a charming Japanese legation lady who was making heroic efforts to master the mysteries of American feminine dress. She was visiting a lady who had a large collection of engravings of the famous Madonnas of the old masters. Her hostess was explaining the peculiarities of the various artists and in doing so called attention to the round-neck dress which most of the Madonnas wore. Suddenly the face of the Japanese lady lit up with joyful intelligence, and she exclaimed: "Oh, yes. I see! 'Tea gown'!"

I had the rare pleasure of meeting Sir James Barrie several times during a visit which he made

FRIENDS OF MANY KINDS

to this country in the early days of the World War. A more modest, unassuming person I have never known, or a more winning one. He talked very little, but invited talk in others by being a "good listener." I sat opposite to him one evening at a dinner of a dozen or more literary personages who had been invited to meet him and another English author who was his companion. As we sat down to the table an animated dispute arose between several of the guests as to the character of a man of international reputation well known to them. One of the guests assailed this person's character violently, calling him a bounder and a rascal. The others defended him, saying he might have made mistakes, but was a fine fellow in spite of them. Barrie sat perfectly quiet, apparently paying no heed to the wrangle. When there came a lull, he said in a low voice and with a quizzical smile, not looking up from his plate: "He was an infernal scoundrel, but 'twas his only fault!" The wordy storm was not resumed.

A delightful companion and joker was Bishop Clark, of Rhode Island, one of the best loved and most useful churchmen of his day in New England. I knew him only slightly in my college days, but subsequently I met him often, usually at men's literary and other dinners. On one of these occasions when I was seated opposite to him, as cigars were being passed and he was cutting the end of one, he said, in thorough episcopal manner: "Mr. Bishop, there are two virtues which lead to self-righteousness. One is early rising and the other is abstinence from the use of tobacco. I am glad to see that you smoke."

Bishop Henry C. Potter, of New York, used to tell a similar anecdote of Bishop Eastburn, of Massachusetts. He was dining for the first time with the Bishop in the latter's house: "After dinner the Bishop fidgeted in his chair in a manner that betrayed, plainly enough, his discomfort, and springing at last from his seat, went to the sideboard and seized a box of cigars. Turning toward me as he did so, and remembering, I suppose, that I was the son of one who, as a college professor, had been widely known for his hostility to tobacco, he exclaimed, with a lugubrious expression which I can never forget, 'Doctor Potter, I presume that you don't smoke?' 'Whenever I can get a chance, I do,' I answered promptly. Whereupon his whole face broadening into a smile of delighted surprise, he exclaimed: 'Thank God! I was afraid that you had inherited the detestable prejudices of your father!' "

FRIENDS OF MANY KINDS

Bishop Clark was sitting one day with a friend in a small hotel parlor when a man entered and began to play vigorously upon the piano. The Bishop's friend, who was a kindly soul, said during a temporary interruption of the tumult: "Bishop, I've heard worse playing than that." The Bishop, who was reading a newspaper, peered over the top of it and asked fiercely: "Where?"

A niece of his of whom he was fond had a very large family of children. As he was leaving one day after a call, she said: "Oh, don't go yet. You haven't seen my last baby?" "I never expect to," he exclaimed as he hurried off.

The Bishop was fond of telling anecdotes about occurrences in his parish. One of these that I recall related to a clergyman who was a famous character in his day. He lived in the era when buttons were made of various kinds of metal and some of them were about the size of the old copper pennies. It frequently happened that many of these, with their eyelets flattened down, were found in the contribution boxes, they making a noise when dropped in similar to that of pennies. The clergyman met the situation by announcing:

"The usual collection will now be taken. Persons desiring to contribute buttons will please not hammer down the eyes, for while that process does not enhance their value as coin, it impairs their usefulness as buttons."

My personal acquaintance with William M. Evarts was very slight, but John Hay, who had a great admiration for him, talked so frequently of him and his witty sayings that I seemed to know him intimately. Hay, who was one of the best talkers I have ever known, always gave the first honors in that blessed field to Evarts, declaring that he not only invariably said in every gathering the best thing that was uttered but said it with the air of one who could say far better things if he would take the trouble to do so. One of the good things I have never seen quoted. It was told to me by the late William B. Hornblower, who had it from his brother, an architect of Washington. Justice Gray, of the Supreme Court, was showing Mr. Evarts over his new house in Washington. As the inspection ended, Evarts asked who the architect was. The Justice replied: "Hornblower was the architect, but I have meddled with his plans so much that he refuses to own it." "Ah," said Evarts, "then you will put on the cornerstone: *Hornblower fecit; Gray interfecit.*"

The fine Evarts spark of wit remained till nearly the end of life. When he was sitting blind

FRIENDS OF MANY KINDS

and almost helpless in his New York home, it is related that Thomas B. Reed, Speaker of the House of Representatives, called on him for a friendly visit. The time was soon after the war with Spain and the acquisition of the Philippines. Reed had been bitterly opposed to acquisition and being full of the subject he talked volubly on it. Evarts listened for a time, and then said: "Reed, I don't think I care to hear more about the Philippines. I'm not going *there* anyway." To another visitor who had tried various subjects without getting response and who had asked if the affairs of the world no longer interested him, Evarts replied: "No, the only world whose affairs interest me is the next one, and nobody who comes here appears to know anything about that."

Abram S. Hewitt I had some acquaintance with when he was a member of Congress from New York City. He was a very able man, an economist of the first rank, and one of the few men that have gone to Congress from New York who fitly represented the intelligence, and financial and commercial supremacy of the great metropolis. After he became Mayor of New York our acquaintance developed into intimacy and I saw him frequently, sometimes because in my capacity as a journalist I had criticized certain of his official acts. On one such occasion when I called on him in the Mayor's office he greeted me in anything but a genial manner. Motioning me to a chair he leaned down and took from the bottom drawer of his desk a copy of the paper with which I was connected. Unfolding it he pointed to an editorial article and said: "In my opinion that is the meanest editorial ever written for a newspaper." It was a severe criticism of one of his appointments to office. I looked him straight in the eye and said: "Don't let us have any misunderstanding, Mr. Mayor. I wrote it." "I thought you did," he said.

I defended my action, and we discussed the subject with some heat for a time, but gradually we calmed down, for he was a man with whom one could talk frankly, and we soon reached a basis of amity. We drifted into a general discussion of public affairs in which I mentioned President Cleveland, who was then in office. "Grover Cleveland?" exclaimed Mr. Hewitt, "why he is the greatest master of platitudes since George Washington!" In his enjoyment of his own epigram, the Mayor fairly leaped from his chair, slapping his legs with delight. A few

FRIENDS OF MANY KINDS

minutes later a man was spoken of who had been a complete failure as a public official. "Oh, Blank," said the Mayor, "the trouble with him was that he was never so undecided as when he had made up his mind!"

The most striking characteristic of Grover Cleveland, as disclosed to me in the few confidential talks I had with him, was frankness. He talked with unrestrained freedom about men and things and about himself. This trait seems to have been so habitual with him that it was revealed from time to time in public utterances which did not increase his popularity with his political associates, as, for example, when he spoke of Congress as a body that he "had on his hands." I once took a Democratic politician from the Pacific Coast to call upon him during the interval between his two terms in the Presidency. The visitor had been a firm supporter of Mr. Cleveland and had been very desirous of making his acquaintance. Mr. Cleveland talked with literally appalling frankness about members of his own party, including several living on the Pacific Coast, expressing very poor opinions of many of them. As we came away from the interview, the politician said: "Now I understand him. He has always been something of a puzzle to me, but I see now where his strength lies—he doesn't give a damn!"

Some time later than this interview I passed an evening with him at his home in New York City. It was in 1891, soon after he had written his letter on the silver question in which he had come out squarely for the maintenance of the gold standard. I told him that I had been watching with great interest the reception given to the letter by Democratic newspapers throughout the country and had been surprised by the small amount of adverse criticism it had aroused. He said, as nearly as I can recall his words and I am sure that I give the substance accurately:

"Well, I have been tempted to say something of the kind for several months, but I refrained because I knew if I said it there would be a cry raised: 'Oh, he wants to be President again!' Now, Bishop, I've been President, and a man who had it once is not overanxious to have it again. But the time seemed to have arrived when I ought to speak and so I let 'em have it." Then, with a complete change of manner, and with a twinkle in his eye, he grasped me by the knee and in a confidential tone said: "Bishop, you'll find there's some pretty good politics in that letter too!"

FRIENDS OF MANY KINDS

And there was, for it secured for its writer a unanimous nomination for the Presidency and a triumphant re-election a year later.

During the same evening Mr. Cleveland spoke of his action, while Governor of New York, in vetoing the five-cent fare bill applying to the elevated railway companies of New York City. Again I quote from memory:

"I was convinced that the bill was wrong, that it was unjust and might lead to practical confiscation. I had no choice but to veto it, but I had not a doubt in the world that by so doing I was ruining my political career. As I got into bed that night after writing and signing my veto message, I said to myself, 'Grover Cleveland, you've done the business for yourself to-night.' The next morning I went down to the executive office feeling pretty blue, but putting a smiling face on it. I didn't look at the morning papers, didn't think they had anything to say that I cared to see. I went through my morning mail with my secretary, Dan Lamont, pretending all the time I didn't care about the papers but thinking of them all the time just the same. When we had finished I said, as indifferently as I could, 'Seen the morning papers, Dan?' He said yes. 'What have they got to say about me, anything?' 'Why yes,

NOTES AND ANECDOTES

they are all praising you.' 'They are! Well, here, let me see them.' I tell you I grabbed them pretty quickly and felt a good deal better."

CHAPTER XI

MAJ.-GEN. GEORGE W. GOETHALS

AS Secretary of the Panama Canal Commission I was for seven years in intimate personal association with General Goethals, the builder of the Panama Canal. I place this supreme credit upon him deliberately, for reasons which I shall state presently. Throughout the period of active construction I was a constant observer of his official acts, of the methods by which he met and solved the problems which pressed upon him incessantly for consideration, thus becoming familiar with the intellectual and moral qualities which form the basis of what is called character and which constitute the personality of a man.

It is customary to regard the construction of the Panama Canal as an engineering achievement, but it was in equal, if not in larger, degree an achievement in administration. The engineering problems were comparatively simple, being those of magnitude, the solution of which followed clearly defined and well-established scientific lines. The problems in administration were new and there were no precedents in American experience from which to obtain light for guidance.

The Canal force was referred to frequently as being in the position of an army in the field. The parallel was only partial. An army in the field is under the absolute control of its commanding general from the moment of its departure for the scene of action. This control is the established order of the military system and is unquestioned. The Canal force, like an army, was in the field, two thousand miles from its base of supplies, but when assembled on the Isthmus it was an army of civilians, and there was no established authority for its absolute control by the man at its head. Every member of it knew this. Not only did the rank and file know it, but the subordinate officials knew it. Experience was to show that it was among the latter, rather than among the former, that the most strenuous opposition to absolute control by one man was to be manifested.

Not only was it an army of civilians, but its duties were civil, not military, and covered a wide and diversified field. In order to construct the Canal it was necessary to create an American state in the heart of a Central American repub-

MAJ.-GEN. GEORGE W. GOETHALS

lic, with a civil government, schools, courts, churches, police system, post-offices, and taxation and revenue systems. This civil government, distinct from engineering control of Canal work, was exercised over one of the most heterogeneous populations ever assembled anywhere on earth, comprising at its maximum about sixty-five thousand souls, and made up of many and widely differing nationalities—North Americans, Spaniards, Italians, West Indians, Greeks, Armenians, Central Americans, and others. To unite in one the two forms of government—engineering and civil—over this population and make it autocratic was no slight problem in administration, and so to exercise that autocratic rule as to make it not only acceptable and effective but popular was a task certainly not inferior to that of the actual construction of the Canal itself.

What was needed, in fact, for the accomplishment of the gigantic work which the United States Government had undertaken on the Isthmus of Panama was a man at the head who was both a great engineer and a great administrator. This rare combination—for few engineers possess large administrative ability—was found in Colonel Goethals. (I shall give him in this narrative the rank which he held at the time.) He

NOTES AND ANECDOTES

had not been long on the Isthmus before he made it apparent that both as an engineer and as an administrator he stood in the first rank. He revealed himself almost at once as that rare product of nature, the born leader of men. From the outset he took his place in a class by himself, and he held it, without dispute or question, till his task was completed. There were among his official associates able engineers and men of trained ability in other professions, but he alone possessed in the supreme degree which the case demanded the qualities of leader and administrator.

It might be said that many generations had fitted him for his great task. The history of the family dates back to 860, in which year one Honorius left Italy with the Duke of Burgundy for France. In a fight with Saracens, Honorius was struck across the neck with what was capable of proving to be a deadly blow, but because of the fine quality of his armor and the physical strength of his person no injury was caused. His escape won for him the title of "Boni Coli." Certain lands were given to him in the north of France, now forming Holland and Belgium. His nickname was translated into the native tongue as "Goet Hals," meaning, as it had in Italian, "good neck" or "stiff neck," and in course of time

MAJ.-GEN. GEORGE W. GOETHALS

it was united in one word and became the family name. The family divided, part settling in Belgium and part in Holland. Colonel Goethals is descended from the Holland branch, both father and mother being Dutch. His parents migrated from Holland to the United States, and he was born in Brooklyn, N. Y., on June 29, 1858. (The name has been Americanized and is pronounced Go-thals.)

The Goethals family, in both Holland and Belgium branches, has contained many members who have achieved distinction in professional and public life, and the ancestral quality of "stiff neck" has persisted with its pristine rigidity unimpaired to the present day.

With the blood of this ancestry in his veins young Goethals entered West Point Academy, from which he was graduated in 1880, standing second in his class. He was retained there as instructor in practical astronomy for a few months, when he went to Willett's Point, remaining there in the Engineering School of Application for two years. After two years' service as chief engineer on Government work in the Department of Columbia, which includes the States of Idaho, Washington, and Oregon, and one year in similar work on the Ohio River, where he was

NOTES AND ANECDOTES

in charge of dikes and dams, he returned to West Point, where he served as assistant instructor and assistant professor in civil and military engineering for four years. During the next five years he was on duty in Tennessee, part of the time in charge of the Elk River division of the Muscle Shoals Canal, and later of all improvements on the Tennessee River from Chattanooga to its mouth. Then for four years he was on duty in Washington as assistant to the chief engineer of the United States Army.

When the Spanish War broke out he went to Chickamauga as chief engineer of the First Army Corps, under Major-General John Brooke, going with him to Porto Rico, where he remained till the taking over of the island by the United States in the fall of 1898. He then returned again to West Point as instructor in military engineering, remaining there till the fall of 1900, when he was promoted to major and was ordered to Newport, R. I., to take charge of fortifications and river and harbor work. When the general staff of the army was organized, in the summer of 1903, he was selected for detail to that and was in that service when appointed by President Roosevelt chief engineer of the Panama Canal and chairman of the Canal commission.

MAJ.-GEN. GEORGE W. GOETHALS

While on duty at Porto Rico he jostled severely the old heads in both army and navy services in command there by a manifestation of independence and plain common sense which was without precedent in their experience. He had been put in command of a detachment, with orders, under protection of a war-vessel, to construct a wharf upon which to land supplies for troops. The wharf was to be made on a beach over which a heavy surf was breaking. Near by were some flat-bottomed barges which the war-vessel had captured and was holding as prizes of war. Major Goethals directed his men to take one of these, fill it with sand, and sink it as the foundation for a wharf. This they did very quickly, and under his direction they were seizing a second one with which to complete the structure when an aide from the admiral in command of the war-vessel appeared with orders from the admiral not to use the barges.

Major Goethals informed the aide that he was acting under the orders of his commanding officer and would take none from any one else, proceeding rapidly with operations with the second barge. The aide reported to the admiral and returned with word that unless the major heeded his orders the admiral would open fire on him. The major told him to fire away. The admiral did not open fire, but appealed to the major's commanding officer. The latter sent word to the major not to use the barges and to get lumber with which to finish the wharf. The major replied that there was no lumber to be had, and finished the structure with the barges, over which he landed the supplies. He was threatened with court-martial proceedings, and was compelled to exist for several years under the acute displeasure of the admiral, who during that period refused to speak to him, but he was never brought before court-martial.

Colonel Goethals entered upon his duties on the Isthmus under very delicate conditions. The force was composed entirely of civilians and had been collected and controlled by civilians. The change from civil to military direction had caused much uneasiness, and this had been aggravated by persistent rumors to the effect that militarism in extreme form would mark the new régime. Had Colonel Goethals been a soldier of the martinet type, complete demoralization would have followed closely upon his advent. Happily he was far from being anything of the kind. In fact, it is doubtful if there could have been found in the regular army of the United States at that time another officer as willing as he was to lay aside his military proclivities and sink the profession of soldier in that of engineer. Soon after his arrival he appeared in ordinary civilian dress before an assembly of the American members of the force, many of whom had expected to see him in military uniform, and in a brief speech he dispelled at once in large degree the uneasiness and alarm which had been created. He declared that there would be no more militarism in the future than there had been in the past, and that no man who did his duty would have cause to complain because of it. This assurance he lived up to absolutely, and no complaint of militarism was heard, because nothing of the kind was visible.

During his entire service Colonel Goethals was never seen in uniform. This was not only a surprise to the members of the force but to his military associates as well. Left to themselves, most of the latter would have worn uniform on gala and public occasions, if not while on regular duty, and for a time some of them did, but his example was too forcible to be ignored and gradually it was followed by all. A secretary of war who visited the Isthmus to inspect the Canal work expressed great surprise because the Colonel was in civilian dress, saying: "I expected to find you in uniform."

"I never wear it," said the Colonel. "I think I shall order you to," said the secretary. With a bland smile the Colonel said: "That won't do any good; I have none on the Isthmus."

It would be difficult to overestimate the beneficial effect of this simple proceeding. It was so simple that many other persons than a secretary of war were not able to perceive its supreme importance. It set a standard of work that was above all tests save that of efficiency, and in his choice of subordinates the Colonel lived up unvaryingly to that standard. The civilian who was faithful and competent needed no uniform to strengthen his position, and the army man who was unfaithful or incompetent learned soon that his uniform was no protection from censure or transfer to other duty.

One of the most conspicuous examples of the Colonel's unmilitary policy was the selection of a civilian, Mr. Sidney B. Williamson, as head of one of the three great divisions of Canal work. At the head of the Atlantic and Culebra divisions he placed two army members of the Canal commission, Colonel Sibert and Colonel Gaillard, but in selecting a head for the Pacific division he passed by all army officers in the force and appointed Mr. Williamson. Here again he fol-

MAJ.-GEN. GEORGE W. GOETHALS

lowed a course which it is doubtful if any other army officer in his position would have had either the courage or the foresight to take. I use the words courage and foresight advisedly, for the act displayed both. It was fully justified by results. Mr. Williamson by his energy and ability set a pace for work which compelled the army officers in charge of similar operations in the Atlantic division to do their utmost to keep up with him both in quality and quantity and also in economy. There was thus created a spirit of rivalry between the two divisions which was of almost incalculable advantage to the progress of the work.

I once asked Colonel Goethals why he selected Mr. Williamson for a position of such importance —what his reasons were for thinking him equal to the task. His reasons, as given to me in reply, throw such clear light upon his methods of judging men and selecting agents that they are worth citing here. While he was in charge of work on the Muscle Shoals Canal in 1889, Major Goethals, as his rank was then, had directed a foreman to sink a test pit in order to find rock foundation for a lock. He had told the foreman that he would have to pass through a layer of quicksand and had warned him to take precautions against a cave-in. The foreman failed to follow directions and a cave-in was the result. The Major discharged him, and Williamson, who was employed at some distance on another job, was recommended for the place. The Major sent for him and put him in charge. Going to the spot on the following day, he found Williamson down in the pit with a gang of negroes shovelling sand into buckets to be hauled up. Later he had Williamson to dine with him and said to him that he did not think he should have gone down into the pit to work side by side with his men, that the place for a foreman was outside and in command of his gang. Williamson said: "You want to get down to rock, don't you?" "Yes." "Well, those negroes were so scared by the cave-in that they refused to go into the pit unless I went with them."

When the job was finished satisfactorily Major Goethals told Williamson, in reply to his request for employment, that he would like to retain him in his employ but he had nothing to offer him except the position of assistant lockmaster, which paid only $40 a month, and he supposed that was not worth his while. "I wasn't asking for money but for a position," said Williamson. "When a man has a wife and child to support he

MAJ.-GEN. GEORGE W. GOETHALS

takes whatever is offered him and holds it till he can get something better."

When Colonel Goethals was placed in charge of Canal construction, Williamson applied for service under him, and the Colonel, mindful of his capacity and character, assigned him to the important position which he filled with great credit to himself and with signal benefit to the entire work.

While giving no outward show of his military profession, Colonel Goethals quietly and firmly put into operation the fundamental rules of military discipline, the chief of which was strict obedience to orders. He had been in control but a few days when a superintendent in charge of a branch of Canal work called at his office and requested to see him. He was admitted at once, and the following conversation ensued:

"I received your letter, Colonel." "My letter? I have written you no letter." "Yes, a letter about that work down there." "Oh, you mean your orders?" "Well, yes; I thought I'd come in and talk it over with you." "I shall be glad to hear your views, but bear in mind you have only to carry out my orders; I take responsibility for the work itself." A few incidents of this kind sufficed to spread the information throughout the

NOTES AND ANECDOTES

force that the work was not to be carried forward by town-meeting debate, but in strict obedience to the orders of the man at the head.

An illuminating example of the beneficial effects of this system was brought to my personal attention about four months after the Colonel had taken charge. I went to the Isthmus in August, 1907, after two years' service as secretary of the Canal commission in Washington. Secretary Taft had given directions that a house be constructed for my use, and Colonel Goethals had ordered the head of the building department to erect it within three months. Six weeks of that period had expired and only the foundations had been placed. I called the Colonel's attention to the matter and he went with me to the site of the building. Calling the foreman of the work to him, he said: "You are in charge of this job?" When the foreman replied that he was, the Colonel said: "You understand that this house is to be finished and ready for Mr. Bishop on the 15th of November?" The foreman, accustomed to the easygoing methods which had prevailed hitherto, replied: "We'll do our best, Colonel." "Then you do not understand," came the quick response, in the quiet, firm voice that the Colonel used throughout the interview; "this house is to be done and

MAJ.-GEN. GEORGE W. GOETHALS

ready for Mr. Bishop on the 15th of November." Turning about, the Colonel walked away.

The foreman, realizing that something quite unusual and important had happened to him, followed quickly, hat in hand, and said: "It will be done, Colonel." And it was. The house was finished and turned over to me, complete in every detail, on November 14. It was a two-story structure, containing a dozen or more rooms, and it had been built in thirty-six working days. The regular period of construction for houses of similar type, previous to that time, had varied from four to six months. In this instance as in all others the Colonel made no threats of any kind as to what would happen in case of failure to obey orders. He did not need to, for the inevitable consequence of failure was known to all.

The effect of this quiet but inflexible control upon the force, and consequently upon the progress of the work, was little short of marvellous. It was soon realized that if the Colonel insisted upon exercising absolute power he assumed also full responsibility. It was also realized that he was master of his business and that all his orders were based upon full and accurate knowledge. Thus it came about that the wisdom of his acts was universally admitted, and discussion about them practically ceased. With discussion and faultfinding there vanished from the force the chief sources of discontent. Then, too, the Colonel was "on the job" every minute. He showed on every occasion exact and intimate knowledge of every phase of the work, for there was no part of it that escaped his personal attention. He spent part, often the whole, of the day in the field, and his evenings in his office. No man in the force worked longer hours than he, and no one of them had the minute and comprehensive knowledge which he not only possessed but had at his command at all times. His ability to master and retain detailed information was at once the marvel and the despair of every one associated with him.

I remember distinctly the exhibition which he made of this faculty before the Committee on Appropriations of the House of Representatives on their first visit to the Isthmus in 1908. At its first session he took the stand and the members of the committee, each equipped with pad and pencil, began a cross-fire of questions at him, most of them betraying a simple ignorance that was quite impressive. The Colonel endured it for a few minutes, and then he suggested deferentially to the chairman that perhaps they could get on more rapidly if he were to outline the condition of the work as it existed. The suggestion was adopted, and the Colonel, in a quiet, deliberate manner, began a narrative of what was proposed and what had been done. As he proceeded, one by one the pencils were laid down, the pads were pushed aside, and the members leaned forward in absorbed attention. When he finished, after about thirty minutes of speaking, the chairman moved over to where I was sitting and said in a low tone: "Good Lord, we've got to give that man what he asks for—he's past master of his business!"

Like demonstration was made at every subsequent visit of a congressional committee. It was the custom of the Colonel to sit by the side of the division engineer or department official who was testifying. Invariably, when a question was asked concerning some detail that the witness was unable to answer, the Colonel answered it for him, showing that he was more familiar with the details of the division or department than the head of it himself.

Occasionally members of the committee would endeavor to show that their own knowledge was possibly superior to his, but the result was always disastrous to the congressmen. At one session,

NOTES AND ANECDOTES

after an hour or more had been consumed in an effort to ascertain whether or not the Colonel had adopted the most economical plans for securing the material for concrete in the locks, a member of the committee, of the "smart Aleck" type, with pencil poised above a pad, turned a sharp eye on the Colonel and proceeded:

Member. How much cracked stone do you allow for a cubic yard of concrete?

Colonel. One cubic yard.

Member. You don't understand my question. How much cracked stone do you allow for a cubic yard of concrete?

Colonel. One cubic yard.

Member. But you don't allow for the sand and cement.

Colonel. Those go into the spaces among the cracked stone.

The Colonel's aspect was "childlike and bland" as he revealed, so clearly that his questioner was able to perceive it, that the able statesmen who had been trying to instruct him in the concrete business were ignorant of the elementary principle of its composition. No further questions were asked him on the subject, and the damaging calculation that the congressman with the pad had evidently intended to spring upon him was withheld from view.

MAJ.-GEN. GEORGE W. GOETHALS

A similar display of superior wisdom was made by a close associate of the victim of the foregoing incident. The second performer belonged to the swagger type, who obviously believed that bad manners were the outward and visible sign of real statesmanship. He habitually cast his gaze about the room previous to asking a question, in order to call attention to the awful exhibition he was about to make of the witness, and then proceeded to interrogate him as if he were a rascal and a thief who was endeavoring to conceal his guilt. On this occasion the question of food supply was under inquiry and the head of the commissary department was on the stand. The item of vegetables was mentioned. Alert and keen-eyed, pencil in hand, pad in readiness for notes, Mr. Swagger asked what vegetables were brought to the Isthmus. A list was given, including cabbages.

Member. What do you charge for cabbages?

Commissary Head. Two cents a pound at present.

Member. Yes, yes; but how much a head?

Commissary Head. That depends on the size of the head.

(Side remark of a cynic in the room: "Measure the size of Mr. Swagger's head and get the average.")

NOTES AND ANECDOTES

Colonel Goethals had a way of his own in dealing with congressmen of this type which caused them to handle him with care after a few experiences with it. He was invariably courteous, but when pushed to the limit he was able to "get even" with them in a manner that they did not soon forget. During the visit of one large delegation its members made a tour of inspection of the various types of commission houses, arriving finally at the one occupied by the chairman and chief engineer. "Let's go up-stairs and see how he lives," said one of them. After going through the rooms another member said to the Colonel: "Pretty fine house! What did it cost?" "It was built by my predecessor, Mr. Stevens," replied the Colonel, stating its cost. "You apportion the quality of the house to the salary the man receives?" was the next question. "Yes," replied the Colonel. "Then, if we were down here working for the Canal we would each get a house half as good as this, the house of a $7,500 man?" said the congressman. "Oh, no," retorted the Colonel with a beaming smile, "if you were down here working on the Canal you would not be getting $7,500."

The Colonel's smile was famous on the Isthmus, being put in use usually to temper the wind of disapproval to the unhappy victim of it. It was thoroughly frank and even beatific in character, but under cover of it he uttered the most deadly of all jests—those that are based on truth. It may be said of it that, like the bass drum in a country band, it covered a multitude of sins.

One other sample of its use may be cited. A visiting congressman, of the chronic double-breasted-coat type, while on a tour of inspection of the locks in the early period of construction, climbed up one of the eighty-two-foot iron ladders that were embedded in the lock-walls, at the imminent peril of being hit with concrete from the buckets that were flying about. Coming safely down, he strutted over to where the Colonel stood with the other members of the delegation and, slapping his bulging chest, asked: "What degree do you give me for that, Colonel?" With the smile in full play, the Colonel replied: "D. F."

There were occasions when the Colonel did not employ the smile in the presence of questions and comments by visitors. High official comment was frequently disconcerting. One cabinet member, who was visiting the Canal and to whom the Colonel had devoted himself continuously for ten days, said on departing: "Colonel, I wish to thank you heartily for your hospitality and your courte-

NOTES AND ANECDOTES

ous attention. I came here all worn out mentally and I shall go back refreshed. You have given me a complete mental rest."

Another official of like rank said, as he was passing in a launch through the nine miles of the Culebra Cut, looking at the banks on either side, which had been seven years in the making and were from one hundred and fifty to two hundred feet in height above the bottom of the Canal: "It is extraordinary, Colonel, that nature should have given these banks on both sides the same slope!"

One of the most frequent of the ignorant questions asked by visitors was in regard to the dams and locks on the Pacific side. A congressman who had passed over the line of the Canal from the Atlantic entrance to the southern end of Culebra Cut at Pedro Miguel, and had heard the full explanation which had been given to all the members of his party, said: "But, Colonel, I don't see why you have these locks and dams on this side. Why don't you sail right out into the Pacific?" There is a tradition that after having this inquiry addressed to him on several occasions, the Colonel with a perfectly serious face replied: "That would be all right, you know, going out, but coming back vessels would have to go up-stream against the current."

MAJ.-GEN. GEORGE W. GOETHALS

The pre-eminent gifts of Colonel Goethals as an administrator were demonstrated in many ways, but most conspicuously in two directions: first, in his really marvellous capacity for mastering and retaining details, and, second, in his ability to win the confidence and inspire the loyalty and enthusiasm of the rank and file of the force. His mastery of details was not confined to the engineering part of the work, but included all departments of civil-government administration and the operation of the Panama Railroad. He showed himself to be one of those rare persons whose mental vision is not hampered by full knowledge of details. He used that knowledge as the foundation for a broad general view of the field of action, with every portion of which he was familiar. He was not only able to see all phases of the problem as it existed, but to foresee the questions that would arise in the future and prepare to meet them. He displayed in rare degree the gift of sagacity without which there can be no successful leadership.

In his dealings with men his chief weapons were frankness, simplicity and fairness as absolute as he could make it. In his first speech, to which I have alluded in the early part of this chapter, by saying that any one in the force could go to him

NOTES AND ANECDOTES

at any time he paved the way for what became later his famous Sunday morning court, with its doors wide open to all comers. This institution was itself a master-stroke in administration. It not only won for him the confidence and loyal devotion of the force, but it gave him intimate knowledge of everything that went on in that force, knowledge of what made for discontent and what made for contentment, and, what was of far greater importance, knowledge of the capabilities and conduct of all the subordinate officers in the organization. This knowledge of detail was an aid to wise administration the value of which could not be overestimated.

His intimate and universal knowledge became a cause of wonder and, at times, of dread. An employee who thought he had not received fair treatment decided to call on the Colonel and state his case. He described the interview as follows: " 'What is your grievance?' asked the Colonel, as soon as I got into his room. I stated it, and when I had finished he pushed a button and told the clerk who answered to bring my record. The clerk brought in a lot of papers with a slip, and the Colonel read it off to me. I was mighty glad I had told him no lies, for everything I had done was there. He talked the whole thing over with me and when we got through I saw I had no grievance. Oh, he's square, I tell you. He talks the thing right out with you and doesn't dodge."

Two Canal workers were overheard talking on a railway-train. One was praising the Colonel, with whom he had had an interview at one of the sessions of the Sunday morning court. The other listened until the narrative was ended, when he said: "Well, I have never met the Colonel personally—never said a word to him or he to me—I don't give a damn for him—*but he's all right!*"

It was a part of my duties to investigate through a special inspector all complaints made by the common laborers, especially Spaniards and other Europeans, concerning their treatment by gang foremen and others in authority over them. By far the greater number of these complaints were of the use of profane and abusive language by the gang foremen. Sometimes this treatment led to small strikes, the men refusing to work longer under an offending foreman, and at other times it was made the basis for a request to be transferred to some other boss. I reported the matter to the Colonel, saying I thought it desirable that something be done to remedy it, since it was a cause of discontent and, consequently, of reduced efficiency, as a dissatisfied and surly force would not give its best effort, but just as little as possible. He replied that he agreed in that view and added that a foreman who thought such treatment the only way by which to direct his gang thereby confessed his incompetence; and a few days later he issued the following:

Culebra, C. Z.,
August 14, 191

Circular No. 400.

The use of profane or abusive language by foremen or others in authority, when addressing subordinates, will not be tolerated.

GEO. W. GOETHALS,
Chairman and Chief Engineer.

This circular was reproduced in the newspapers of the United States and was headed, in one instance, that came to my notice, "Sunday-school Methods on the Canal." It was nothing of the sort, for it was not an order in the interest of morals but in the interest of efficiency. Its effect was instantaneous. Complaints ceased at once, several foremen were reduced to an inarticulate condition for a time, but there was no instance of violation of the edict. This was one of the many instances of the Colonel's minute attention to every detail of administration, the aim always being the same—efficiency.

MAJ.–GEN. GEORGE W. GOETHALS

The time came when the open, just treatment of all stood Colonel Goethals in good stead. In February, 1911, a formidable effort was made to organize a strike of all the railway employees of the Canal commission and Panama Railroad which, if successful, would have paralyzed all excavation work. A locomotive engineer on the Panama Railroad, in August, 1910, had allowed his train, in defiance of signals, to run into the rear end of another train, and in the collision the conductor of the latter train was killed. He was tried on a charge of involuntary manslaughter, convicted and sentenced to a year in the penitentiary. An appeal was taken to the Supreme Court of the Canal Zone, and the verdict was confirmed on February 21.

Colonel Goethals was at the time on his way back to the Isthmus from the United States. A mass-meeting of transportation men was held on Sunday, February 25, at which, under the lead of some hot-heads, resolutions were adopted denouncing the verdict as unjust, demanding the liberation of the engineer, and declaring that if the Canal authorities did not free him by seven o'clock on Thursday evening following, the transportation men would leave the service. A delegation from the meeting went in a body to the office of the chief engineer and stated the result of the meeting to the acting chairman and chief engineer, who persuaded them to await the arrival of Colonel Goethals before taking action. On Thursday following, Colonel Goethals arrived and went at once to his office. A leader of the protesting employees called him up by telephone at ten minutes past seven and asked him if he had received the petition, when the following conversation took place:

Colonel Goethals. No, I have received no petition.

Leader. You haven't? Has not Colonel Hodges advised you of the action of our meeting?

Colonel Goethals. Yes, I have been advised of a demand from a mob.

Leader. When will we get our answer?

Colonel Goethals. You have it now.

Leader. We have it? I have not received it.

Colonel Goethals. Yes. You said if the man was not out of the penitentiary by seven o'clock this evening you would all quit. By calling up the penitentiary you will learn that he is still there. That's your answer. It is now ten minutes past seven.

Leader. But, Colonel, you don't want to tie up this whole work?

MAJ.-GEN. GEORGE W. GOETHALS

Colonel Goethals. I am not proposing to tie up the work—you are doing that.

Leader. But, Colonel, why can't you pardon the man?

Colonel Goethals. I will take no action in response to the demand of a mob. Furthermore, I cannot act in this case at all because you yourselves placed it in the hands of President Taft when he was on the Isthmus a few weeks ago. He told you then that if the Supreme Court confirmed the verdict he would consent to consider the case. It is in his hands now.

Leader. Must the man stay in the penitentiary till he acts?

Colonel Goethals. So far as I am concerned he must. As for your threat to leave the service, I wish to say to you and to your associates, that every man of you who is not at his post to-morrow morning will be given his transportation to the United States and there will be no string to it. He will go out on the first steamer and he will never come back.

Leader. Suppose one of us should be sick?

Colonel Goethals. It is an unfortunate time to be sick.

Only one man failed to be at his post the next morning, and he sent a doctor's certificate saying

NOTES AND ANECDOTES

he was too sick to be there. The mail of the chairman and chief engineer's office was stuffed with letters from signers of the resolutions asking to have their names taken off, and there was not a shadow of a strike.

An amusing sequel to the incident occurred on the following Sunday at a ball game at Ancon. One of the leaders of the mass-meeting who had signed the threat to leave the service and return to the United States, where, according to the resolutions, he could "enjoy the protection of the Constitution," approached the plate to bat. As he did so a clear voice from the grand stand cried:

"What, you here! We thought you had gone back to the United States to enjoy the Con-sti-tu-tion!" A roar of laughter followed, and the poor fellow was not able to get within hailing distance of the ball either then or afterward, for his every reappearance was greeted with the same query, roared in joyful chorus from the entire assemblage. The Colonel had got the laugh on the would-be strikers by his straightforward and indisputably just handling of the affair and nothing more disastrous than that could happen to them.

The Colonel's custom of spending a part of each day, usually the forenoon, in visiting the work, gave him a knowledge of every part of it that often caused a rude shock to some subordi-

MAJ.-GEN. GEORGE W. GOETHALS

nate official whose performance was not quite up to the mark. No such official could foresee when the Colonel in his personal railway motor-car, known because of its color as the "Yellow Peril," might appear on the scene; neither could he foresee what defect or shortcoming the keen eyes of the chief engineer might detect.

Toward the end of the task, when completion ahead of time was assured, a tendency to relax effort became visible in several quarters, due partly to lessened tension and partly to a desire to make the job hold out as long as possible. In one such instance the Colonel appeared suddenly on the spot and called the foreman in charge to account for slowness. The foreman said: "Oh, that's all right. I have one hundred days in which to complete the job." "That's not the way I work," replied the Colonel. Returning to his office he sent for the foreman's superior officer and told him the work must be pushed more rapidly. A few days later he revisited the work and saw that his order had not been obeyed. He then issued an order transferring the work from the official who had charge of it to his personal direction, and directing that the plant be removed to a different location on the Canal line and consolidated with another.

The official who had been in charge of it and

who was retained under the Colonel's personal direction called upon him, saying that unless the transfer order was either revoked or modified he should have to resign, as it overruled him, adding of the order that it could not be obeyed because it would cause friction between the two forces, and the men would refuse to be transferred. "Send the men to me," said the colonel; "I am the best handler of friction on the Isthmus." The men called on the Colonel and retired from the interview content to be transferred. The official again protested that the order could not be obeyed because the tools were not at the new location. "When were you at the old place?" asked the Colonel. "Yesterday morning," was the reply. "I had a special train at the old place," continued the Colonel, "at three o'clock yesterday afternoon. All the tools and the men were taken on it to the new place. I had arranged with the chief quartermaster to provide quarters for them, and they are all installed there now."

The official, showing visible agitation, declared that unless the order taking the work from his supervision were revoked or modified he saw nothing for him to do but resign. "As for resigning," said the Colonel, "that is a matter for your personal decision, but the order will neither be

MAJ.–GEN. GEORGE W. GOETHALS

revoked nor modified." The official resigned, and the general comment on the incident was one of astonishment that a man who had served seven years under the Colonel knew him so slightly as to think that he would revoke or modify an order he had once issued.

The faculty of going surely and directly to the vital point of a matter was displayed in a remarkable degree by Colonel Goethals. So also was the gift of plain speech. While inspecting the work in progress under an associate official he rebuked him sharply for disobedience to orders, saying his conduct amounted to disloyalty. The official unconsciously confessed judgment by saying: "I can be loyal to you." "You *can be* loyal," retorted the Colonel; "then you have not been!" "I am told," continued the official, "that you have accused me of disloyalty and have said that a man who is disloyal will lie and steal?" "So he would," said the Colonel, "given provocation."

The Canal commission had club-houses in six of the largest settlements along the line of the Canal, but there was none at Ancon. These contained, among other features, billiard and pool rooms and bowling-alleys. When the building at Culebra was removed because threatened by the slides in the cut, employees at Ancon petitioned

NOTES AND ANECDOTES

Colonel Goethals to have the bowling-alleys placed at Ancon. They offered, in case the commission should be willing to defray the cost of moving and housing them, to assume the cost of maintenance. The commission chaplain at Ancon gave cordial support to the proposal and called upon the Colonel one day to report progress. "The boys held a meeting last night," he said, "to consider the question. They were very enthusiastic and authorized me to say to you that if the commission would defray the cost of removal and housing they would support the alleys to the full extent of their power." "What is your power?" asked the Colonel, and the whole plan collapsed. The chaplain, after stammering for a moment, admitted that he could not say what the power was worth.

The management of the commission club-houses had been placed at the outset under the Y.M.C.A. of the United States because that institution had a trained and experienced force for the work. Under the rules of the association no games of any kind were permitted in the club-houses on Sunday, although the club-houses were open on that day. The result of this was that many employees did not become members of the clubs because, Sunday being their only holiday, they wished to enjoy themselves as much as possible.

MAJ.-GEN. GEORGE W. GOETHALS

Colonel Goethals was an earnest advocate of full privileges on Sundays, but he was opposed by the national committee of the Y.M.C.A. in the United States, who threatened to withdraw their workers from the Isthmus if such privileges were granted.

A visiting member of the national committee, in discussing the subject with the Colonel, said: "Now, Colonel, how many employees do you estimate go, as you say, into objectionable places in the cities of Panama and Colon on Sundays because they cannot play billiards, pool, bowling, and other games in the club-houses on that day?"

"The answer to your question," said the Colonel, "which every member of a Christian church who believes in its tenets must make is, that if by keeping *all* the club-houses open fully on Sunday *one* man could be kept away from those places, the opening would be justified."

When a question arose as to individual responsibility in a committee on an international matter with the Panama Republic, one member of the committee being absent in the United States, a member present said he thought the committee could not safely assume the responsibility of the absentee. Colonel Goethals, who was a member, said: "Oh, that's all right. I'll take the responsibility for two."

A Panama government official, on the eve of

NOTES AND ANECDOTES

what threatened to be a tumultuous and possibly riotous political campaign for a presidential election, sought an interview with the Colonel and said he was afraid of riot and bloodshed unless some moral influence was exerted by the Canal authorities in favor of order—meaning in favor of his own political party. The Colonel said cheerfully: "Well, we have the Tenth Infantry out here on the line. If you wish me to do so I will order it to march into Panama at any moment!" "Oh, no, no," exclaimed the official, "I don't think it will come to that!"

A Washington visitor met Colonel Goethals one day in my office at Ancon. The Canal was at that time nearing completion. "How soon are you going to be able to pass ships through the Canal?" he asked. The Colonel replied that he had no doubt that he would be able to pass them in 1914. The visitor, paying little heed to the statement, continued: "Colonel, I come in contact in Washington with many of the diplomatic representatives of foreign governments with whom I am on quite intimate terms. They say such things as this to me: 'You know that the Canal will never be open to navigation. You know that the Gatun dam will not hold water. You know that the slides in Culebra Cut can never be stopped. You know that the locks can

MAJ.-GEN. GEORGE W. GOETHALS

never be operated.' Now, Colonel, what shall I say in reply to these people?" The Colonel, with an amused gleam in his eye, said quietly: "I wouldn't say anything."

That was his habitual answer to ignorant or malicious criticism. Whenever an instance of it was brought to his attention and a suggestion was made to publish a refutation of it, he would say: "Oh, let it go. We will answer them all later—with the Canal." He was as indifferent to fulsome praise as he was to ignorant and unjust blame, and cared so little for both that he rarely or never read anything that was written about himself. On several occasions, when writers of the gushing type had sent to him in advance of publication, for approval, articles about himself and his work, he brought them to me to read for him, with the injunction to cut out mercilessly all "fool" references to his personal appearance or conduct, holding me to strict accountability for failure to obey orders in any respect. His sense of humor is acute and unfailing, and he has the quite unusual ability to enjoy a joke at his own expense. He was hugely amused by a conversation which he overheard concerning himself on a Panama Railway train. Two men were talking in a seat directly behind him, neither of them having recognized him. One, a foreman, was telling the other, who was a visitor, of the great things he and other foremen were doing in building the Canal, repeatedly referring to the Colonel as the "old man." When he had finished, the other said: "But what does the old man, as you call him, do?" "Oh, he just comes around and looks over what we've done."

His dislike of "fuss" of all kinds, official or other, amounted to a passion. There was never any parade or demonstration about anything he did, and his suffering was visibly acute when anything of the sort was thrust upon him. The proceedings in Washington and New York in 1914, when various societies conferred medals of honor upon him, caused him an amount of genuine anguish which he described as "awful." He permitted no blare of trumpets, no demonstration of any kind, when the Gamboa dike was blown up on October 10, 1913, and the water was let into Culebra Cut; none when the first vessel passed through the Gatun locks on September 26, 1913; none even when the Canal was thrown open on August 15, 1914, to the commerce of the world. On none of these epoch-marking occasions was he visible in the forefront of things. He was not on the prow of the first tug that passed the locks, but on and within the lock-walls studying closely the working of the machinery of the gates and

MAJ.–GEN. GEORGE W. GOETHALS

valves. He was not on the bridge of the first ship to pass from ocean to ocean, but on the lock-walls and along the banks of Gatun Lake and the sides of Culebra Cut, watching both the operating machinery and the wave-action created by the moving vessel.

What other man in his position would have been capable of this complete self-effacement? An English diplomatic official, who was a passenger on the first ship to go through the entire Canal from the Atlantic to the Pacific, wrote of it to a friend: "Colonel Goethals did not go through. He saw us off at Cristobal, and then appeared on the locks at Gatun and Pedro Miguel. At the latter point John Barrett made arrangements to raise three cheers for Colonel Goethals, but directly it started, the Colonel, who was in shirt-sleeves, turned his back and ran. John was left cheering."

Finally, as the supreme revelation of the character of the man whose personality I have been endeavoring to portray, I am permitted to quote from a letter which he wrote in May, 1913, to a congressman who had introduced in the House of Representatives a bill providing for his promotion to the rank of major-general in the United States Army as reward for his services in building the Canal:

NOTES AND ANECDOTES

"I feel that I should make my position clear in respect to the proposed measure so far as it or similar legislation may apply to me. I am not insensible to the honor to be conferred upon me by the bill and appreciate the motives friendly to myself which inspired its introduction. It is also to be assumed in addition to the personal side, that the action contemplated may be regarded as a mode of expressing satisfaction that the Canal work has thus far been successfully prosecuted. Nevertheless, it has always been my position that the army officers assigned to the Canal are amply compensated, not only by the additional pay they received, but by the honor of being associated with the undertaking, and we are but performing our duty in devoting our best energies to the successful prosecution of the work. It must be remembered that those of us who are members of the Commission are receiving three times the amount of our regular army pay and are at the same time doing nothing more than that for which we have been educated and trained by the Government. According to my view, we are not deserving of recognition or reward for our services here, and I do not think that myself or others of the Commission should be singled out for honors.

MAJ.-GEN. GEORGE W. GOETHALS

"Neither do I think that army officers should receive any special consideration for their services here in contradistinction to the civilian employees. Several civilians have occupied positions of great responsibility on the work—notably Mr. S. B. Williamson, former division engineer of the Pacific division—and I cannot speak too highly of the splendid service that himself and civilian employees in general have rendered. These employees are not asking for rewards for their labors other than the pay received in their various positions. I see no reason why myself or other service men should be regarded as in a class by themselves and selected for benefits by special legislation, and, in my opinion, such favoritism should not be extended. Therefore, while deeply gratified at the evidence of your good-will as expressed by the introduction of the measure, it suggests itself that I ought to acquaint you with my views upon the subject, and I trust in so doing you will not consider me inappreciative of your kindness.

Yours sincerely,
GEO. W. GOETHALS."

But this manly letter had no effect upon Congress. All the army and navy officers who had

NOTES AND ANECDOTES

been three years or more in the Canal service were rewarded with promotion, but no reward of any kind was bestowed upon the civilian employees although Congress is a body of civilians. The full injustice of this discrimination is realized when one considers that the army and navy officers receive old-age pensions when they are retired from the service, and that the civilians, many of whom had passed the best years of their lives at Panama, severing all their connections in the United States, were faced, on their return to their country, with the necessity of finding new employment under very unfavorable conditions.

INDEX

Abou Ben Adhem, 112
Adams, Brooks, 163
Adams, Charles Francis, 161; his opinion of diary writing, 162, 163; his love of contradiction, 162, 165; and Wayne MacVeagh, 165
Adams family, the, 162, 163
Adams, Henry, 163; his estimate of Roosevelt, 121
Adams, John, 162
Adams, John Quincy, 162, 163
Albany, Assembly Chamber at, 169
Aldrich, Thomas Bailey, 10
"Alice in Wonderland," 143
"American Commonwealth," by James Bryce, 169, 170
"Ancient Irish Sagas, The," article by Roosevelt, 140
Andrews, James Petit, 2
Anecdotage, the inventor of the word, 1-6
Anti-Slavery Standard, the, 15

Bankruptcy court-room, motto for, 168
"Banty Tim," by John Hay, 46
Barnes libel suit, the, 153
Barrett, John, 225
Barrett, Wilson, 161
Barrie, Sir James, 176, 177; *anecdote:* "his only fault," 177
Bayle's Dictionary, 71
Becket, Tennyson's, 157
Beecher, Henry Ward, preaching of, 35-37; his Friday evening prayer-meetings, 39, 40; his voice, 42; at Horace Greeley's funeral, 43; *anecdotes:* effect of sermon on a woman, 37; bald-headed sinners, 37; remedy for sleeping in church, 38, 39; Westerner who doubted his orthodoxy, 39, 40; women speaking in meeting, 40; pitted against Doctor Chapin, 41-43
Belgians, the, enslavement of, by Germany, 171
Bennett, James Gordon, 100, 127
Bigelow, John, his "Retrospect of an Active Life" quoted, 32
Birrell, Augustine, quoted, 6
Bishop, Joseph Bucklin, Secretary of Panama Canal Commission, 124 ff., 129 ff., 187, 200; assault upon, by politicians, 125; the *Herald's* attack upon, 126-128; house of, on Isthmus of Panama, 200, 201
Blaine, James G., 72; E. L. Godkin's opposition to, 103, 104
Bonaparte, Charles J., 129
Boswell, James, 5, 6
British Embassy at Washington, the, anecdotes of, 173-175
Bromley, Isaac H., 51; and Clarence Cook, 9; humor of, 68 ff., 81; known as "Ike" Bromley, 68; on *Tribune* editorial staff, 69 ff.; William Winter's tribute to, 70; his quick perception of humbug, 70, 71; his Caleb Cushing article, 74-76; his "Logan on His Feet" article, 76; his famous "Punch, brothers, punch with care" poem, 77-81; quoted on the editorship of *The Evening Post*, 96; *anecdotes:* Bayle's Dictionary, 71; a Blaine election bet, 72; General Burnside, 72; on a Sound steamer, 72; his class in college, 73; the lyre and Ed-

INDEX

mund Clarence Stedman, 73; Mr. Congdon's theology, 73, 74; the mystery of life and death, 82; William Winter's melancholy, 83
Brooke, Major-General John, 192
Brooks, Noah, 53, 78
Brown University, 8
"Brown, Winkelried Wolfgang," fictitious name of I. H. Bromley, 80
Browning, Robert, 60
Brownsville, Texas, the riots at, 140, 141
Bryant, William Cullen, 15
Bryce, James, his "American Commonwealth," 169, 170
Burnside. General Ambrose E., 72

Carnegie Hall, Roosevelt's last speech at, 145
"Castilian Days," by John Hay, 44
"Cave Canem," article by I. H. Bromley, 74-76
Century, The, Roosevelt's article in, 140
Chapin, Dr. E. H., 35; pitted against Henry Ward Beecher, 41-43
Choate, Joseph H., 16, 162; success of, as after-dinner speaker, 166-168; on enslavement of Belgians by Germany, 171; *anecdotes:* "Depew Natural Gas Company, Limited," 167; Chauncey M. Depew's substitute, 168; motto for Bankruptcy Court, 168; the discourteous judge, 168; falling ceiling of Assembly Chamber, 169; literary piracy case, 169-171
Claflin, Tennie C., 26
Clark, Bishop, 177; *anecdotes:* two virtues, 178; piano playing, 179; the last baby, 179; buttons in contribution box, 179
Cleveland, Grover, 120, 122; frankness of, 183; his letter on the silver question, 184; his veto of five-cent-fare bill, 185
Club-houses of Panama Canal Commission, 129-132, 219-221
"Conductor when he receives a fare, the," I. H. Bromley's poem, 77-81
Congdon, Charles T., 21, 73, 74; his account of Horace Greeley and the draft riots, 11-15
Congress, Panama Canal visited by committees from, 202-208
Conkling, Senator Roscoe, 54, 56
Cook, Clarence, 9
Courts, Sunday morning, on Isthmus of Panama, 210
Crane, William H., 161
"Crumbs of Comfort," editorial by J. R. G. Hassard, 31, 32
Culebra Cut, Panama Canal, 208, 224
"Curiosities of Literature," by Isaac Disraeli, 2, 4
Cushing, Caleb, I. H. Bromley's article on, 74-76

Dana, Charles A., 100, 160, 161
Delmonico's, dinners given by Henry Irving at, 158-161
Depew, Chauncey M., 167, 168
DeQuincey, 3
Disraeli, Benjamin, 1-3
Disraeli, Isaac, 2-4
Draft riots, the, 11-16
Dunne, Finley Peter, 152

Eastburn, Bishop, 178
Elevated railway five-cent fare bill, veto of, 185
Evarts, William M., 61; John Hay's admiration for, 180; *anecdotes:* Justice Gray's new house, 180; the next world, 181

INDEX

Evening Post, the New York, 15, 86; under editorship of Edwin L. Godkin, 87 ff., 102

Fairchild, Oliver, 49
Fashion, the ship, 49
Foraker, Senator, 140

Gaillard, Colonel, 196
Gamboa dike, the, 224
Garfield, President, 54; assassination of, 55-57
Gatun locks, Panama Canal, 224
German Embassy at Washington, anecdote of wife of attaché of, 175
Gibbons, John S., 15, 16
Givens, James, 48, 49
Gladstone, William E., 58, 61
Godkin, Edwin L., editor-in-chief of *The Evening Post*, 87 ff., 102; personal characteristics of, 87, 88; his daily conferences, 89; his writing, 90 ff.; his delight in "journalistic rows," 92-95; his sense of humor, 94 ff.; his power to wound, 94; intellectual youthfulness of, 94; "Jakery and Mikery" his designation for corrupt politics, 95; associated with Carl Schurz and Horace White, 96; as editor of *The Nation*, 99; charge of omniscience against, 99 ff.; a "great editor," 100, 102, 110; unusual intellectuality of, 100, 101, 109; optimism of, 103 ff.; his feeling toward commercial journalism, 103; his fight against Blaine, 103, 104; his faith in American people, 104; his comment on Lowell's address on the Independent in politics, 104; courageous hopefulness of, 105; his ideas of political reform, 105-107; his attitude toward the Spanish War, 107; his loss of faith in American institutions, 107-109; called a pessimist, 109; *anecdotes:* the son of an Irishman, 96; the reformer in municipal politics, 97; his treatment of bores, 97, 98; effective treatment of critics, 98, 99
Godwin, Parke, 160
Goethals, Major-General George W., builder of the Panama Canal, 187 ff.; autocratic power to, 133, 134; ancestry of, 190, 191; a born leader, 190; name of, 190, 191; education and engineering service of, 191, 192; appointed chief engineer of Panama Canal and chairman of Canal Commission, 192; at Porto Rico, 193, 194; unmilitary policy of, 194-196; uniform not worn by, 195; strict obedience required by, 199; questioned by Congressional Committees, 202-208; mastery of details by, 202-205, 209, 210; his smile, 206, 207; his Sunday morning court, 210; profanity among Canal workers stopped by, 211, 212; indifference to unjust criticism, 222, 223; modesty of, concerning achievements, 224, 225; attitude toward reward for services in building canal, 225-227; *anecdotes:* use of barge for wharf foundation, 193; a secretary of war and the Colonel's uniform, 195; selection of S. B. Williamson, 196-199; the Colonel's orders and his responsibility, 199; hastening the building of Mr. Bishop's house, 200; cracked stone in concrete, 204; price of cabbages, 205; houses and salaries of Canal workers, 206; the degree of D.F., 207; the banks of the Culebra Cut,

INDEX

208; locks and dams on Pacific side of Canal, 208; employee with a grievance, 210; threatened strike of railway employees, 213-216; the foreman who wished to delay work, 217-219; official accused of disloyalty, 219; plea for bowling-alleys at Ancon, 219, 220; Sunday closing of club-houses, 221; taking responsibility for two, 221; riotous political campaign and the Tenth Infantry, 222; the Colonel's answer to critics, 222, 223; a foreman's idea of the Colonel's part in the work, 224; the Colonel runs away from his cheerers, 225

Goldsmith, Oliver, 24

Gray, Justice, 180

Greeley, Horace, 45, 69, 100; editorship of *The Tribune* by, 10 ff.; personal appearance of, 10, 11; besieged by reformers and intellectuals, 10, 26; his action during the draft riots, 11-16; his method with troublesome callers, 17-19; an "easy mark" for beggars, 19, 20; his handwriting, 22; inaccuracies not tolerated by, 21, 22; personality of, 23, 28; power as an editor, 24; Presidential campaign of, 25-33; campaign photograph of, 27; not qualified for Presidency, 28; defeat of, 29; letters of, quoted, 29, 30, 32; his wife's death, 30; return of, to *Tribune* office, 30; indignation over "Crumbs of Comfort" article, 31, 32; death of, 33; funeral services of, 42, 43; *anecdotes:* retorts to two irate visitors, 17-19; lady requesting contribution to charity, 19; inaccuracy in statement of election returns, 21; of his handwriting, 22

Hamlet, Beerbohm Tree's performance of, 84

Harte, Bret, 10, 171; writings of, 46, 47; credited with "Little Breeches," 47; a cowboy's appreciation of, 172, 173

Hassard, John R. G., 9; "Crumbs of Comfort" by, 31, 32

Hay, John, 9, 123, 171; quoted on value of anecdotes and letters, 5, 58; tribute of, to Beecher, 43; in American diplomatic service in Europe, 44; his "Castilian Days," 44; on editorial staff of *The Tribune*, 44, 45, 50-53; his "Pike County Ballads," 45-49; his dislike of journalism, 51; as temporary editor-in-chief of *The Tribune*, 53-57; Thayer's "Life" of, quoted, 54; his letter-writing, 57, 58; his feeling toward countries of the Spanish Main, 58, 62; Tom Taggart in his "Mystery of Gilgal," 59; death of his eldest son, 59; his conversation a "joy forever," 60-62, 67; his death, 66, 67; Roosevelt's tribute to, 66; his admiration of William M. Evarts, 180; letters from, 49, 59; *anecdotes:* of burning Mississippi steamer and "Jim Bludso," 48; "I've been going for them kings again," 51; Puritan consciences, 52; "Books in the running Brooks," 53; the situation after Garfield's assassination, 55-57; envoys from countries of the Spanish Main, 62; Jones and his "secret mission," 62-64; the anti-imperialists and the Philippines, 64, 65; on death of political foe, 65; Lincoln and an office-seeker, 65, 66; the Adams family, 163

"Heathen Chinee," by Bret Harte, 46

232

INDEX

Herald, the New York, attacks on J. B. Bishop by, 126-128
Hewitt, Abram S., 181-183; disapproval of newspaper article by, 182; on Grover Cleveland, 182
Hornblower, William B., 180
"Horse-car Poetry," 80
House, built for J. B. Bishop on Isthmus of Panama, 200
"Hunting of the Snark, The," 143

Irving, Sir Henry, intellectuality of, 156; dinners at Delmonico's given by, 158-161; *anecdotes:* his performance of *Becket,* 157; Wolsey's "Farewell," 157; the dying theatrical manager, 158; no after-dinner speeches, 159-161; comments on *Rivals* and *Hamlet,* 161

Jakery and Mikery, E. L. Godkin's designation for corrupt politics, 95
Japanese legation, a lady of the, and dress of Madonnas, 176
Jefferson, Joseph, 42
"Jim Bludso," by John Hay, 45, 48, 49
Johnson, Doctor Samuel, 4-7; quoted, 5, 24
Johnson, Oliver, 12, 13
"Jones," and his secret mission, 62-64

Kipling, Rudyard, luncheon to, 172

Lamont, Dan, 185
Le Bon, Gustave, quoted, 69
Lincoln, Abraham, 57; and office-seekers, 65, 66; Lowell quoted on, 155
"Literary Nightmare, A," by Mark Twain, 79

"Little Breeches," by John Hay, 45, 47
"Logan on His Feet," by I. H. Bromley, 76
"Lothair," by Benjamin Disraeli, 1
Lowell, James Russell, quoted, 105; on E. L. Godkin's writing, 90; on omniscience, 101; his address on "The Place of the Independent in Politics," 104; his tribute to Godkin, 109; on Lincoln, 155
"Luck of Roaring Camp, The," by Bret Harte, 46, 172
"Lunatic Fringe of Reform," Roosevelt's opinion of, 112

MacVeagh, Wayne, 162, 165
Madonnas, dress of, and Japanese lady, 176
McKinley, William, 119
Miller, Joaquin, 10
"Mollycoddles," Roosevelt's feeling toward, 112
Morley, Lord, his estimate of Roosevelt, 111; effect of Roosevelt's conversation on, 122-124; his definition of political oratory, 144, 145
Muscle Shoals Canal, the, 192; 197, 198
"Mystery of Gilgal, The," by John Hay, 45, 58, 59

Napoleon, Lord Morley's comparison of Roosevelt with, 123
Nation, The, called "The Weekly Judgment Day," 99
National Publishers and Booksellers Association, banquet of, 41
Neilson, Adelaide, 84
North American Review, The, Lowell editor of, 101
Norton, Charles Eliot, 109

INDEX

Oratory, political, Lord Morley's definition of, 144, 145
Osgood, James R., 46
Overland Monthly, The, 46

Pacifists, Roosevelt's opinion of, 112
Paine, Albert Bigelow, 80, n.
Panama Canal, the, construction of, 187 ff.; Colonel Goethals given autocratic power in building of, 133, 134, 189 ff.; administration problems of, 188 ff.; Goethals appointed chief engineer of, 192; visits of Congressional Committees to, 202–208; opening of, to world commerce, 224; discrimination by Congress against civilian workers on, 228
Panama Canal Commission, J. B. Bishop secretary of, 124 ff., 129 ff., 187, 200; club-houses and books secured by, 129–132, 219–221; Colonel Goethals chairman of, 192
Panama Railroad, arrest of engineer on, 213–216
Paris Peace Conference, Wilson's commissioners for, 147, 148
Parker, Commissioner, 113–115
Pepys' Diary, 163
Philippines, the, 64, 164, 181
"Pike County Ballads," by John Hay, 45–49
"Place of the Independent in Politics, The," 104
"Plain Language from Truthful James," 46
Platt, Senator, 140
Plymouth Church, 36
Political oratory, Lord Morley's definition of, 144, 145
Porto Rico, 192, 193
Potter, Bishop Henry C., 178
Profanity in Canal Zone, stopping of, 211, 212

"Punch, brothers, punch with care," 77–81

Raymond, 100
Redfield, J. S., 11
Reed, Thomas B., 117, 181
Reid, Whitelaw, 27, 32, 53, 54
"Retrospect of an Active Life," by John Bigelow, quoted, 32
Revue des Deux Mondes, "Le Chant du Conducteur" in, 80
Ripley, Dr. George, 9
Rivals, the, 161
Rogers, Samuel, 3; quoted on melancholy, 83
Roosevelt, Quentin, 148
Roosevelt, Theodore, 64; his tribute to John Hay, 66; humanness of, 111 ff.; Lord Morley's estimate of, 111; and Commissioner Parker, 113–115; friendships of, 116; his dislike of flattery, 116; gift of foresight, 118; on his election to the Vice-Presidency, 118; his comment on his work as Police Commissioner, 118; his succession to the Presidency, 119 ff.; called "pure act" by Henry Adams, 121; a tireless talker, 121–124; election to the Presidency, 122; compared with Napoleon, by Lord Morley, 123; energy of, 123, 124; intimate personal relations of J. B. Bishop with, 124; his comments on assault of politicians on J. B. Bishop, 125–127; pleasure of transacting official business with, 128; rapidity of mental processes, 129; club-houses and books on Isthmus of Panama secured by, 129–132; sole responsibility in building Panama Canal given Colonel Goethals by, 133, 134; comments on persons he disliked, 138–140; his ability to

INDEX

concentrate, 140; and the Brownsville affair, 140, 141; wide reading of, 141–143; political oratory of, 143–146; story of his public life proposed by, 146; in hospital, 147, 149; courage under affliction, 147; on the commissioners for the Paris Conference, 147, 148; his feeling in regard to Presidential candidacy for 1920, 148, 149; his "Letters to His Children," 149–151; his love of children, 152; his letter-writing, 152–154; personality of, 154; *anecdotes*: his a boy's mind, 113–115; reading of Western tour lectures, 116; discovery of the Ten Commandments, 117; daily greeting of visitors in Cabinet Room, 135–138; naval candidate for promotion, 139; an office-seeker and "The Hunting of the Snark," 143; original views in history, 142; "I liked my job," 144; his last speech, 145

"Roosevelt's Letters to His Children," 149–151

Root, Elihu, 148

Russian-Japanese War, the, 164, 165

Schurz, Carl, 96
Scribner's Magazine, Colonel Goethal's article in, quoted, 133
Scribner's Monthly, I. H. Bromley's article in, 80
Seward, William, 2
Sheridan, General, 146
Sherman, General, 85
Sibert, Colonel, 196
Silver question, the, Cleveland's letter on, 184
Sinclair, Samuel, 20
Socrates, his "Apology" quoted, 106

Spanish Main, the, 58, 62
Spanish War, the, 107
Stedman, Edmund Clarence, 10, 73; quoted, 93, 94
Stoddard, Richard H., 10

Taft, William H., 123, 133, 134, 215; on the anti-imperialists and the Philippines, 64
Taggart, Tom, character in "The Mystery of Gilgal," 58, 59
Taylor, Bayard, 9
Terrapin, anecdote concerning, 175, 176
Thackeray, 166
Thayer, William R., his "Life of John Hay" quoted, 54
"Theodore Roosevelt and His Time," by J. B. Bishop, the writing of, 146, 147
"Through the Looking Glass," 143
Tilton, Theodore, 26
Tree, Beerbohm, 84
Trevelyan, Sir George Otto, Roosevelt's letter to, quoted, 120; tribute of, to Roosevelt, 121
Tribune, The, 96; editorial office of, in 1870, 8–10; Horace Greeley editor of, 10 ff., 24, 30; in the draft riots, 11–16; reply to *The World* concerning Greeley and the draft riots, 14; "Crumbs of Comfort" editorial in, 31, 32; "Jim Bludso" published in, 45; Bret Harte's stories in, 46; John Hay editorial writer for, 50–53; Hay editor-in-chief of, 53–57; I. H. Bromley on editorial staff of, 69 ff.; "Cave Canem" quoted from, 74–76; "Logan on His Feet," quoted from, 76; William Winter dramatic critic of, 82
Twain, Mark, 49, 71; his "Literary Nightmare," 79, 80

INDEX

Victoria, Queen, 60
"Virginian, The," by Owen Wister, 172

Warner, Charles Dudley, 10; *The Nation* called "The Weekly Judgment Day" by, 99
Washington, Booker T., 174
Washington society, anecdotes of, 173-176
Western, The, Latin version of "Punch, brothers, punch" in, 80
White, Horace, 96
Wilkes, John, 3
Williamson, Sidney B., 196-199, 227
Wilson, Woodrow, 162, 164, 165; his commissioners for the Paris Peace Conference, 147, 148

Winter, William, 9; his tribute to I. H. Bromley, 70; dramatic critic of *The Tribune*, 82; the poetry of, 83; melancholy of, 83; his criticism of Beerbohm Tree's *Hamlet*, 84; Adelaide Neilson's gift to, 84; story of darky preacher told by, 85; letter from, 86
Wister, Owen, his "Virginian," 172
Wolsey's soliloquy, 157
Wood, Fernando, 74, 75
Woodhull, Victoria, 26
World, The, 13, 14

Y. M. C. A., club-houses of, in Canal Zone, 220, 221
York, the Archbishop of, 144